CW01467679

FULL EMPLOYMENT FOR EUROPE

The Commission, the Council and the Debate on Employment in the European Parliament 1994-95

Ken Coates MEP

and

Stuart Holland

*Together with the Coates Reports on
an Action Plan on Employment Policy
&
a Coherent Employment Strategy for the European Union*

SPOKESMAN

for

EUROPEAN LABOUR FORUM

First published in Great Britain in 1995 by
Spokesman
Bertrand Russell House
Gamble Street
Nottingham, England
Tel. 0115 970 8318
Fax. 0115 942 0433

British Library Cataloguing in Publication Data available on request from the British Library.

ISBN 0-85124-579 X cloth
ISBN 0-85124-580 3

Printed by the Russell Press Ltd, Nottingham
(Tel. 0115 978 4505)

CONTENTS

Preface

by Ken Coates and Stuart Holland

Part I: How it happened

When I was elected to the European Parliament in 1989, I found myself precipitated into the office of Chairman of the Sub-committee on Human Rights. This was a job which engaged my full attention, and which enabled me to follow through many initiatives with which I had been concerned for a long time before my election.

But the problem of unemployment, and particularly of long-term unemployment, was becoming increasingly insistent. Like most Parliamentarians, I met this problem in my Constituency as I struggled with a case load which was fiercely augmented by the closure of coalmines, and by industrial contractions in other industries, 'down-sizing', and bankruptcies. Poverty, hopelessness, and sheer despair ceased to be peripheral conditions and became a 'normal' part of our environment.

Meantime, as we moved into the 'nineties, the European Union was consolidating, the Maastricht Treaty was agreed, and the socialists in the European Parliament began to consider the next steps towards closer union, enlargement of the boundaries to take in new member states, and rationalisation of the internal mechanisms of this more complicated structure.

A Socialist Conference was called at Vilamoura in Portugal. Part of its agenda included institutional proposals. Part concerned whether to change the language structure of the Parliament and other European institutions. But this rather introspective, if important, agenda was shaped at a time in which referenda were beginning to show increasing disquiet and even dissent among the existing member states.

For many years, convergence upon the European Union had not been an unpopular cause. It aroused strong idealism and encouraged a sense of international co-operation. For many people, it had continually been associated with consistent economic prosperity and improvement. But now, mass unemployment was eroding that confidence and seeding widespread alienation and discontent. Crime statistics began to reflect these social maladies. Worse, there was evidence that many people were suffering not only material deprivation, but also loss of hope. In this hostile environment bred new species of nationalism, xenophobia, and even racialism. Right-wing extremist political parties began to expand far beyond their previous limits.

I entered the discussion at Vilamoura at the earliest possible moment, and asked my colleagues to consider whether the fight against unemployment should not become the centre of our political engagement. Unemployment was destroying the health and security of millions of people. It could also erode, block, and ultimately unwind the processes involved in the hard-won approach to political union.

As a result of this intervention, the British section of the Socialist Group, the European Parliamentary Labour Party, invited me to prepare a report on a European Recovery Programme. This I did with the strong help of Dr Stuart Holland, Michael Barratt Brown, and John Hughes, together with Regan Scott of the Transport and General Workers' Union. My report was published in 1992. As a result, President Jacques Delors invited me to discuss some of the issues with his staff.

It was becoming very clear to me that the political parties might be able to refocus their efforts on the question of employment, but that they would make no serious progress until public opinion, including the decisive opinion of those who had kept their jobs, came to support the urgency of resolute action. So emerged the proposal for an initiative which might widen the appeal to such public opinion. It suggested that we should invite the Churches, members of the academic professions, and other opinion formers to create an Assize which could evaluate the proposals which already existed to meet the problem of unemployment, and solicit other suggestions.

President Delors enthusiastically endorsed this idea, and I subsequently approached a very large number of Church leaders, trade unionists, and non-governmental organisations, all of whom gave their support to the idea. Those responding included the Archbishop of York and a number of Anglican clergymen, Cardinal Basil Hume, the Archbishop of Westminster, and the Roman Catholic Bishops of Birmingham, Glasgow and Strathearn, the Apostolic Pro-Nuncio in London, the Cardinal Archbishop of Milan, and a number of Protestant Churchmen from several countries. Distinguished academics offered to help. They included Professor Peter Townsend, Professor Ruth Lister, and Professor Jan Tinbergen, the Nobel Laureate. Support was also promised by a number of trade union leaders including Rodney Bickerstaffe and Gavin Laird of the British Public Employees' and Engineers' Unions.

Several meetings were organised under the joint auspices of the *Commission des Épiscopats de la Communauté Européenne* (COMECE) and the European Ecumenical Commission for Church and Society (EECCS), the two main Associations of European Churches, representing Catholic and Protestants respectively. The Secretary Generals of these two bodies, Noel Treanor and Keith Jenkins, worked tirelessly to ensure that a very large measure of agreement was reached. Unfortunately, the very strong commitment of the Churches could not override the financial difficulties involved in creating an action on the appropriate grand scale. Perhaps these problems will yet be resolved, in the not-too-distant future.

The most extensive meeting took place in Brussels early in 1994, with the participation of some two dozen churchmen, representing the Roman Catholic and Protestant Churches, together with the Greek Orthodox Church. Parliament was debating action against unemployment at the same time, but it proved unable to agree on any of the several resolutions which confronted it. Each proposal in turn was voted down. I am pleased to say that the Church leaders, by contrast, were unanimous in their decisions about the need for action on this issue. I believe that the extensive discussions within this informal forum helped later, when we came to develop the Parliamentary agenda on employment, during the second half of 1994 and the first seven months of 1995.

One of the proposals to come from the Churches was that Parliament should be asked to organise a 'parliament' of unemployed and excluded people.

Very large support came from my own Political Group for this proposal, before the European Elections which took place in June of that year. Subsequently, it was to prove more difficult to turn that support into effective action on the ground.

But throughout this time, I had been agitating for the Parliament to establish a special Committee to deal with this issue. Aspects of the problem were already covered in existing Committees: there is a Committee on Social Affairs and Employment, and another Committee on Economic and Monetary Affairs. But both consider questions of employment within an agenda crowded with other necessary problems. Many other Committees can rightly be seen to touch on employment questions: obviously, unemployment particularly affects young people, and women, both of which groups relate directly to appropriate Committees in the Parliament. There are powerful Regional and Environmental Committees, which also need to consider employment problems and the effects of unemployment. But the virtue of a special Committee would be that it would focus on this issue as its central concern.

In the end, the Socialist Group was persuaded, and secured the agreement of other Groups to establish the Temporary Committee on Employment, which was constituted immediately after the June 1994 Elections. Mrs Celia Villalobos Talero, representing the Christian Democratic European Peoples' Party, was elected President, and I was elected Rapporteur. That is to say it was my job to originate the reports upon which the Committee itself, and ultimately Parliament, would vote.

What follows is a record of the papers which were generated in this work, beginning with the first proposal for the Committee's Agenda.

This text, and all of those which follow, owes a very great deal indeed to the advice of my friends, Michael Barratt Brown, John Hughes, and Regan Scott. But above all it is in debt to the persistent and unremitting efforts of Stuart Holland, upon whose vision it so evidently depends.

I had been working closely with Stuart Holland for many years, in the field of industrial democracy and economic planning, before he began his pioneering study 'Out of Crisis', which associated twenty-five European scholars in a project for European Recovery. Together we had subsequently sought to persuade political parties and peace movements to explore the need for a Disarmament and Development Initiative, based upon global co-operation. We received a great deal of encouragement from economists and political leaders of various colours, but the end of the Cold War did not bring the necessary co-ordinated action. Yet the need for this kind of co-operation continuously increased, and at the European level, indeed, became more urgent.

The Delors White Paper on *Growth, Competitiveness and Employment* drew on a rich stock of ideas, amongst which these were included. It was therefore a very great pleasure for me to resume my close collaboration with Dr Holland, in seeking to persuade the European Parliament of the necessity for a truly convergent and combined strategy of action for employment.

Two full-scale reports, two debates and two resounding majority votes have made these arguments the property of the European Union and its Parliament. Will they be implemented? If they are, the pursuit of social cohesion will ensure that European Union becomes a process of social liberation, and rising expectations. The fulfilment of the aspirations of millions of people may then be part of the redefinition of our political space.

But if they are not, what then? Will the European Union unravel in a welter of discontents and atavisms?

When Mahatma Gandhi was asked what was his opinion of European civilisation, he responded 'It would be a good idea'. It would indeed, and so would democracy, and both have a possible future. But this will depend on whether we determine to make an end to social exclusion, and to enlist the creative talents of all the many millions who are presently locked outside the productive economy, and outside constructive political space.

Ken Coates

Part II: What it was about

In the debate in June 1989, on my resigning from the House of Commons, many Conservative MPs predictably claimed that this showed that I had little faith in Labour's prospects for government. The late Ian Gow MP told them they were wrong. It was clear to him that, although my destination was Florence, I was going to help Jacques Delors widen his European agenda.

For the first time, the Delors White Paper on *Growth, Competitiveness and Employment* of December 1993 set the European Union an employment target: the creation of 15 million jobs. This was the target range of the high growth scenario of my report to him, a year earlier, on *Economic and Social Cohesion in the 1990s.*[1]

New financial instruments had been designed to help in the new job creation. The European Union would issue its own bonds — Union Bonds — which would be managed by a new European Investment Fund (the EIF). Agreed by the European Council at Edinburgh in December 1992 and featuring in the White Paper, these likewise had been a main recommendation of the report.

The EIF and macroeconomic policy

The rationale for recommending a new Fund and Union Bond was primarily macroeconomic.

First, Europe needs a joint macroeconomic policy which can reinforce that of member states. No European economy, including Germany, is large enough to withstand the pressures of free capital movements and foreign exchange speculation. Neither the UK in the sixties and seventies, nor France in the eighties, was powerful enough to avoid deflationary cuts in social expenditure and employment. Together, especially with a single currency, the member states could be.

Second, the other standard instruments of macroeconomic policy such as exchange rate changes or expenditure financed from national taxation either would be ruled out by a single currency or would involve an increase in the Commission's own resources. Such an increase was unacceptable to national governments. This is one of the reasons why the earlier MacDougall Report has remained a dead letter.[2]

Third, it was already clear that the deficit and debt conditions for a single currency of the Maastricht Treaty would be likely to register deflationary effects on expenditure and employment. These could not be offset by increased national expenditures without further hazarding the conditions themselves.

By contrast, a European borrowing and expenditure instrument — as an instrument of the Union rather than member states — need not count on national public sector borrowing requirements (PSBRs), and thereby could offset such deflationary effects.

In his correspondence with Ken Coates, President Santer has claimed that the Fund never was anticipated as a macroeconomic instrument. This is understandable in view of the manner in which the Fund was presented to and adopted by the Edinburgh European Council meeting.

Michel Sapin, French Finance Minister at the time of Edinburgh, confirmed this at an October 1993 meeting of the Economic Committee of the French Socialist Party which invited me to clarify the arguments on the Fund.

Certainly it may have been impolitic at Edinburgh to advise John Major that the proposed Fund amounted to a new European PSBR. It would have been more effective to stress that the spending on the TENs — the new trans-European transport and information networks — would have to be repaid by borrowers from the Fund rather than financed by the British taxpayer as an increase in the Commission's own resources.

Offsetting the deflationary effects of a single currency

What is more important than the original conception of the Fund and how it was endorsed at Edinburgh is the fact that it now exists as an institution and already has committed a major part of its first borrowing tranche of 8 billion ecu.

To introduce it meant amending the Rome Treaty to enable the Union to borrow and spend on its own account. All of the twelve national parliaments have done this. The three new member states have assigned to it. The instrument is in place with the potential to act as a European borrowing and expenditure mechanism in a manner which could offset deflationary effects from the financial convergence criteria of Maastricht without counting on the PSBRs of member states.

But 8 billion ecu is not enough to register a significant macroeconomic effect. The Fund needs to be expanded on a major scale to do so. This now is urgent granted the scale of the effects of meeting the deficit and debt conditions of Maastricht. Extrapolations from the model of the Economic Council of the Labour Movement (ECLM) in Copenhagen — published in Chapter 10 — indicate that if the heaviest debtors were to fulfil the 60 per cent debt conditions of Maastricht in full, this could lose over ten million jobs. Meeting the deficit conditions could lose another million and a half jobs.

Further, there is a classic Keynesian justification for increasing the borrowing and spending limits of the Fund. Private markets are not ensuring that savings are being translated into investment. In OECD Europe there is an excess of savings over actual investment equivalent to 6 per cent of GDP.

In Chapter 12, his correspondence with Ken Coates, President Santer questions the projected unemployment from fulfilling the Maastricht criteria on the grounds that 'budgetary consolidation would still be necessary even in the absence of the convergence criteria laid down in the Maastricht Treaty'. He also recommends the cases of Denmark and Ireland as evidence that 'budgetary consolidation strategy can go hand in hand with higher, not lower, economic growth and employment'.

Advised by Commissioner de Silguy, Commissioner Bangemann stresses that one gets different results from different economic models. As he puts it in Chapter 11: 'Pure Keynesian-demand models produce the first set of results. Other models, like MULTIMOD, the IMF's international macroeconomic simulation model . . . (give) somewhat different and, in principle, more realistic results'.

However, as argued in Chapter 12, both Ireland and Denmark are very small economies, whose expenditure cuts in the eighties and early nineties registered insignificant deflationary effects on European demand as a whole. A scenario in which most of the member states were cutting deficits and debt at the same time to meet the Maastricht criteria would be very different.

Also, both Denmark and Ireland devalued significantly before or during their phases of 'budgetary consolidation' in a manner which would not obtain for those member states seeking to meet exchange rate convergence as the prelude to monetary union.

Nonetheless, in Ireland unemployment rose by twenty per cent, while long-term unemployment doubled during the adjustment period. This was despite the fact that the economy itself was growing by up to 6 per cent per year, or nearly double that of the most strongly growing member state economies in the current recovery.

The worst recession since the war

In Denmark the 'budgetary consolidation' measures undertaken by the government from the mid 1980s resulted in:
(1) a recession from 1986/7 to 1993 which was the longest not only in the post-war history of the country but also of any industrialised country since the war;
(2) an increase in unemployment of nearly 60 per cent.
The latter is terrifyingly close to the percentage increase in unemployment from debt reduction in my 10 millions extrapolation from the Danish ECLM model, in Chapter 10.

Granted the mutual beggar-my-neighbour effects on most member states seeking to cut budgets and borrowing at the same time, the 10 million lost jobs from debt reduction plus one-and-a-half-million from meeting the annual deficit targets is entirely consistent with what happened in the Danish case. Indeed, it may be an under-statement granted the degree to which Danish unemployment compensation is exceptionally high and long-term, sustaining demand in a manner which would not be replicated in much of the rest of Europe.

The politics of increased unemployment

If registered unemployment were to rise from eighteen to thirty millions as a result of meeting the debt and deficit conditions of Maastricht, the political and social results not only for the European project but also for democracy could be catastrophic.

One of the standard questions for students of modern history is whether the rise of fascism in interwar Europe was due to rising unemployment. The bright answer is to argue that many other factors were at work. The right answer is that it was.

As stressed in Chapter 10, reducing unemployment is arguably the key political issue of the decade because:
(1) racism and political extremism spawn when people either have no jobs, or cannot gain jobs matching their skills, or see their children unemployed or under-employed.
(2) unemployment in the present member states also is a major *foreign* policy issue.

There is much talk of further referendums on whether individual member states should join a single currency. But there is no way in which electorates are likely to sanction either a single currency, or free access for imports from central and eastern Europe, or widening the Union to include not only the Visegrad Four (Poland, Hungary, Czech Republic, Slovakia) but also Bulgaria and Romania if unemployment at the same time increases by up to a half or more.

Spurious realisms

There is a tendency in some circles to dismiss such warnings as exaggerated. This allegedly realistic approach has three main variants.

The first is to argue that monetary union will not happen precisely because the employment costs would be so high.

But, as argued in Chapter 10, this does not square the political circle. If the really heavy debtors are excluded from the project, this means that the Netherlands, Belgium, Sweden and the Mediterranean countries other than France become a 'second tier' of a Europe *divided* rather than united by a single currency.

The second alleged realism is to argue that such countries cannot join now but can join later.

But this does not resolve the underlying problem that their debt reduction still will pose massive political and social costs in terms of higher unemployment if they are to meet the criteria at any time. Meanwhile, the strength of the single currency for those member states which may have ascribed to it will have profoundly destabilising effects on the currencies of the heavy debtors.

The third alleged realism is that recovery has happened since the European Investment Fund was adopted in 1992, and that the Fund no longer is needed as a counter-cyclical instrument.

But this not only ignores the uncertainty of the current recovery. It wholly ignores the deflationary effects of the Maastricht financial convergence criteria as well as the fact that at Cannes it was admitted that there were not enough own resources to make expected contributions to the financing of the TENs, which are *key* investment areas for the 15 million jobs target in the Delors 1993 White Paper.

This is why the arguments in this volume for and around the Temporary Employment Committee should be central to the political debate in Europe. It also is why the 3:1 majority for the second resolution from the European Parliament this summer is politically important.

French support for the Fund

One key member state — France — has consistently supported an expanded role for the Fund. Michel Rocard first called for a 50 billion ecu Fund in his address to the annual congress of the French Socialist Party in October 1993. Within three days, in a press interview, President Mitterrand was asked whether he supported Rocard's call. He replied not only that he did, but that it was such a good idea that its borrowing powers should be doubled to 100 billion ecu. He added that he had checked with Brussels that morning to see if it was feasible and had confirmation that it was.[3]

Challenged in turn on the issue, French Prime Minister Balladur declared that he supported such an increase in the Fund. Employment Minister Michel Giraud did the same in evidence to the Temporary Employment Committee of the European Parliament at the beginning of 1995.

When heads of state and government arrived at Cannes in June and found that there were next to no budget resources to finance the TENs, President Chirac called for an expansion of the Fund to finance them in line with the original conception of the Fund and of the Delors White Paper.

But the wider political base for this does not yet exist. Some heads of coalition governments appear clearly in favour — such as Nyrup Rasmussen in Denmark and Jean-Luc Dehaene in Belgium — but finance ministers are not.

In some cases, the arguments simply may not be understood. Where they have been — as by François Mitterrand and Jacques Chirac — they have prompted demands for a major Fund with macroeconomic potential. This is why the debate was needed in the European Parliament this year and why it should be widened.

Democratising the debate

Such a widened debate cannot only be about macroeconomic instruments. It also is about reducing working time and increasing labour intensive employment, especially in the social sphere. The Council has already endorsed this in principle by adopting the Local Development and Employment Initiatives programme of the Commission at Cannes.[4] Much of this volume, including our own joint contributions, is about these issues.

The debate also must be able to demonstrate to regional and local governments that they can benefit from direct borrowings from the European Investment Fund.

Likewise SMEs stand to gain in a major way if the Fund fulfils the commitment to take equity shares in them within the next eighteen months, and thereby to provide a venture capital market of the kind which Europe hitherto has so notably lacked.

The so-called Surveillance Procedures

In March 1995 the Council in fact agreed to a process by which the debate on the European economy and employment can be democratised on a rolling medium-term basis.

Only some of the press noticed, possibly because of the uninviting title for the process — Surveillance Procedures — suggests covert actions rather than opening up the issues. In fact the new so-called Surveillance Procedures are for monitoring the implementation of Maastricht. But they also are more.

In the 1992 report for Jacques Delors, I argued that one of

the clearest reasons for scepticism or opposition to further European Union was that people felt that major decisions on integrating markets and money were being taken over their heads in an undemocratic manner.

To reinforce democracy at European level I recommended in Chapter 1.2 of the report — *The Democratic Imperative* — that article 103.2 of the Treaty should be invoked as a means of legitimating a rolling half yearly debate on the European economy and employment. Not only the European Parliament but also the Committee of the Regions and Local Government, the Social Partners (separately or together) and ECOSOC — as well as ECOFIN — should be involved.[5]

The European Parliament has echoed this in endorsing paragraphs 32 and 39 of the first draft resolution from the Temporary Employment Committee in December 1994. Paragraph 32 reads that the Parliament:

'Notes also that article 103(2) of the EC Treaty determines that "The Council shall, acting by a qualified majority on a recommendation from the Commission, formulate a draft for the broad guidelines of the economic policies of the Member States and of the Community"; urges the Commission to give priority to the formulation of new guidelines focused on employment creation in the context of the economic upturn'.

Paragraph 39 of the first resolution reads:

'Suggests that the overall monitoring of the action plan be undertaken by the Commission in conjunction with the Social Affairs and ECOFIN Councils, and that the Commission present on a half yearly basis a progress report on the implementation of the Action Plan to the European Council, the European Parliament and the Economic and Social Committee and the Social Partners'.

At Essen, the European Council did not respond to a range of substantive issues in the first report from the Temporary Committee — notably on increasing the resources of the EIF. But in a decision in March this year the Council endorsed the procedures called for in paragraph 39 — adding also the

Committee of the Regions and Local Government to those who should be involved.

The form of the procedures is summarised in the text of Chapter 13, and synthesized in the two figures for the two half yearly procedures.

In practice they can and should be used to sustain pressure for progress on the Action Plan on Employment of the Resolutions from the Parliament. They also could and should include half yearly debates in national parliaments, timed in such a manner that their views can be expressed both before Council meetings and before the European Parliament gives its recommendations to the Council.

Certainly the new procedures offer a major advance on the time when I stood opposite John Major at the dispatch box in ill-attended late night debates on the Commission's budget — rather than the economic policies of member states and the Union — months *after* the budget had been agreed by the Council, and without any chance of influencing the outcome.

An enabling majority vote

If Europe stays blocked on employment then more than a single currency is at issue. If key debtor states raise unemployment to meet the criteria for a single currency the viability of the European project — East and West — is in question.

So what is to be done? Article 103.2 provides for a qualified majority vote. But its use at present is unlikely.

This may change as and when most of the Mediterranean countries other than France realise that they may be excluded indefinitely from a single currency while the Czech and Slovak republics have debt and deficit levels which would enable them to qualify.

It may change more rapidly, granted that there now are pressures not to allow grants under the Structural Funds to those member states which are not making progress to reducing debt and deficits. Such IMF style 'structural adjustment' offers the worst of beggar-my-neighbour deflation with none of the best potential of a European monetary fund such as the EIF.

A way out may be for the Intergovernmental Conference (IGC) to consider a new form of 'enabling majority vote'. Unlike a qualified majority vote, an enabling vote would not bind those who did not support it. But it would enable those who did — possibly on a simple majority — to pursue joint policies on which they were agreed.

In the case of the European Investment Fund this would mean that enterprises and regional and local governments in those member states which voted for an increase in its resources would be able to apply to borrow a share of those increases, while those in the other member states would not.

If this resulted in increased pressure from the Social Partners and the Committee of the Regions and Local Government for a further increase in the borrowing of the Fund, then the new Surveillance Procedures would already in large part have proved their worth.

Stuart Holland
London
August 1995

Footnotes

1. Stuart Holland, *Economic and Social Cohesion in the 1990s*, 1992, later published as *The European Imperative*, Spokesman Books, Nottingham, 1993.

2. Sir Donald MacDougall's own thoughts on this matter are to be found in Chapter 5 of *A European Recovery Programme*, pages 53-61, edited by Ken Coates MEP and Michael Barratt Brown, Spokesman for European Labour Forum, Nottingham, 1993.

3. The fact that President Mitterrand needed such clarification from the Commission that the Fund could be used in this way suggests again that President Santer had some reason for claiming in his correspondence with Ken Coates that the Fund was not originally perceived as a macroeconomic instrument.

4. European Commission, *Local Development and Employment Procedures*, Sec 564 (95), Brussels, March 1995.

5. Stuart Holland, *The European Imperative*, *op.cit.*

PART I

The Agenda for the Temporary Committee on Employment

CHAPTER 1

Agenda for Employment
Ken Coates and Stuart Holland

The European Parliament's Temporary Committee on Employment was constituted immediately after the European Elections in June 1994. Its first full meeting took place in September. This paper was prepared in an attempt to suggest the agenda for the Committee's work, which was scheduled to take one year.

The terms of reference of the Temporary Committee were these:

The European Parliament
1. Decides, pursuant to Rule 135(2) of its Rules of Procedure, to set up a temporary committee on employment, with 36 members;

2. Decides to confer on this committee the following mandate, powers and responsibilities:

This temporary committee shall be responsible for examining all aspects of employment policy in order to develop a coherent strategy for combating unemployment and creating sustainable employment.

In this context, it will monitor implementation of the White Paper on Growth, Competitiveness and Employment. If necessary, it will propose additional or alternative measures.

It will prepare Parliament's position in preparation for the Essen European Council and will monitor implementation of the decisions taken. Its term of office shall be twelve months with effect from July 1994.

The Delors White Paper on Growth, Competitiveness and Employment set out to 'foster debate and assist decision-

making' and began with a clear commitment. 'Why this White Paper?', it asked. 'The one and only reason is unemployment'. Over the last twenty years, it insisted, the European economy's potential rate of growth has shrunk from some four per cent to about two-and-a-half per cent a year. Unemployment has been rising consistently from one trade cycle to the next. There has been a five per cent drop in the investment ratio. 'Our competitive position in relation to the USA and Japan has worsened as regards: employment, our shares of export markets, R & D and innovation and its incorporation into goods brought to the market, and the development of new products'.

The White Paper was published in 1993, following extensive consultations with the member states. A preliminary presentation to the European Council in Copenhagen that summer was the basis for an agreement that member states should send their own proposals for the elements to be included in the White Paper, before the 1st September. This would enable the Commission to complete the necessary work, so that the document would be ready for consideration at the December European Council Meeting.

The resultant White Paper affirmed that it would be necessary to create fifteen million new jobs in the European Union, if unemployment were to be halved there, by the end of the century. This was the point of departure for the Temporary Committee, and the basis of its proposed agenda.

K.C.

*   *   *

The heads of state and government have taken a courageous decision in endorsing the fifteen million jobs target in the White Paper, while some Commissioners have called for even more ambitious targets.

But it is strongly arguable that the problems of competitiveness and employment in the Union are much more severe than is publicly admitted at key levels of government, and some levels in the Commission.

Impending new unemployment

The current economic recovery will not be sufficient to register major falls in unemployment because of structural shifts in the economy, new dimensions to technological unemployment, and revolutionary flexible or lean production techniques which imply halving employment in sectors such as auto components and textiles.

There is evidence that trans-European information networks will both create jobs and cause unemployment. There are major impending job losses in the defence and defence related sectors. Small and medium firms are losing market share both to low wage economies in East Asia and to multinational companies in the internal market.

Because of this, employment creation in the December 1993 White Paper on *Growth, Competitiveness, Employment*[1] has been over-estimated, and further measures will be needed to meet the fifteen million jobs target.

An efficient economy and an efficient society

To fulfil the White Paper jobs target new policies will need to be adopted which achieve both *a more efficient economy* and *a more efficient society.*

An efficient economy is judged by the rate of increase of output per worker and the quality of its products and services. An efficient society should be judged by the rate at which it can decrease unemployment and the efficiency with which it can improve the quality of socially useful production and services.

The revolutionary flexible production techniques pioneered by Japan and already adopted by leading US firms can in some cases double or treble productivity. This is the key to an efficient economy. *If achieved in less than a third of European manufacturing this would return average manufacturing productivity to the levels of the post-war 'economic miracle'.*

Job creation through reduced working time

Although controversial, the issue of reduced working time, or job sharing, should be considered by the Committee. *A reduction of average working time of 2.5 per cent over five years and 3.5 per cent over ten years would create nearly ten million jobs.*

Higher productivity from transition to flexible production means that not all reductions of hours need imply a reduction of pay. It also means higher profits and tax revenues — without raising tax rates — to finance new employment policies. In turn, normal taxes on those firms gaining most from the new productivity could be alleviated through tax concessions aimed to encourage negotiation of shorter working time.

Although reduced working time might in due course imply a Commission directive, such a policy should not simply be imposed from above. It should reinforce the process by which people can negotiate how their personal time is increased; time for family responsibilities to children or parents, re-qualification or leisure. Fuller employment, increased quality in social provision and such widened social choice on working hours are keys to a more efficient society.

Environment, social services, health and education

Environmental reclamation may be high-tech, but also often it is intensive in employment of semi-skilled male labour. There also is considerable scope for job creation in the social sector and in socially useful production and services. A range of such programmes in local services, including improved care for the elderly and the young, has been highlighted in Commissioner Flynn's response to the White Paper.

This implies increasing the number of carers, just as improving quality in health care or social services would mean increasing employment. There also is considerable scope for job creation from reducing class size in most levels of education, as well as special programmes in distance learning, provided that these are backed by local educational and training institutions.

Reinforcing the micro sector: multi-regional and multinational networking

At the microeconomic level, medium sized firms in association with small firm suppliers need to be able to gain some of the features of multinational companies if they are to be able to offset competition both from East Asia and from larger multinationals themselves. Likewise former defence related firms dependent on national budgets and markets need to be able to diversify into civilian markets in a multinational environment.

One of the new ways to achieve this is through multi-regional and multinational *networking* rather than mergers. This implies strategic alliances on joint policies for marketing, mutual product rationalisation, developing new products and processes, mutual exploitation of the new trans-European information networks and joint applications for relevant Union assistance such as the Fourth Framework Programme, the ADAPT programme or the new Objective 4 of the Structural Funds, which can assist their own transition to flexible production.

Macroeconomic implications: making use of the Union and its new financial instruments

The prospects for raising the competitiveness of the Union are positive if more weight can be given to increasing awareness of the efficiency raising potential of transition to flexible production. A 1992 style 'vision' of a changeable future is needed, and an Action Programme imperative if Europe thereby is to defend its remaining hold on parts of the global innovation frontier.

On the other hand, over ninety per cent of the trade of the enlarged Union including the Scandinavian countries will be internal rather than external to the Union. Under such conditions, and with increased productivity in leading export firms, there need not be a balance of trade constraint on employment programmes for the Union as a whole.

Finance Ministers are naturally concerned about the costs of national programmes, not least because of the budget and borrowing limits of the Treaty of Maastricht as a condition for achieving a single currency.

However, through new instruments such as the European Investment Fund and Union Bonds, the Union itself now can finance investments in a manner which (i) can offset pressures on national budget deficits, and (ii) make it more possible to achieve the national budget and borrowing conditions of Maastricht.

Overall, policies for employment need to be *pro*-active over the medium-term rather than simply *re*-active in the short-term. The framework for this is in articles 3a[1] and 103.2 of the Treaty of Maastricht, and should be implemented.

Procedures and evidence

The Committee should consider taking a range of advice in the form of invitations to selected specialists to comment on the issues involved.

The Committee should consult with the Social Affairs Committee to consider the invitation of Employment Ministers from member states to give evidence in response to a range of issues and questions. They may also wish to take evidence from Finance Ministers on their attitude to the new Union financial instruments such as the European Investment Fund and Union Bonds.

Footnote

1. *Growth, Competitiveness, Employment: The Challenges and Ways Forward into the 21st Century*, White Paper, Commission of the European Communities, COM(93) 700 final, Brussels, 5 December 1993.

CHAPTER 2

The New Unemployment

Ken Coates and Stuart Holland

The draft agenda which was presented to the Temporary Committee offered a preliminary groundwork for the analysis of the European unemployment problem. This chapter was originally published together with Chapter 1, but we have taken an editorial decision to separate the two because we think the argument warrants separate attention.

K.C.

I
1.1 Cyclical Unemployment

There already are some voices claiming that growth is recovering strongly in the Union and that new financial instruments to promote investment and employment such as the European Investment Fund are less necessary than when they were agreed in principle at the Edinburgh Summit in December 1992.

These arguments are misguided. Over the last twenty years, the link between investment and jobs has been broken. Thus the economy of Spain doubled in real terms between 1970 and 1992, but employment declined by two per cent.

The growth rates now being achieved by several economies of the Union will be insufficient to create anything like fifteen million jobs. Some economists who support the principle of the White Paper jobs programme nonetheless claim that even three per cent GDP growth over five years may only create some 1.2 million jobs, and only 4 million over ten years with *net* gains against a rising unemployment trend of only 400,000 jobs in five years and 1.5 million jobs over ten years.[1]

Many macroeconomic forecasts are limited by over-aggregation. Nonetheless, such estimates suggest that the job creation proposals which constitute so major a part of the White Paper on *Growth, Competitiveness and Employment* have been over-estimated, as were the Cecchini estimates on the employment generation from the creation of the internal market.[2]

What is needed is a more detailed analysis of the employment creation effects of different parts of the White Paper proposals, and supplementary policies, and examination of the relevant Commissioners and Commission officials in hearings by the Employment Committee.

1.2 Structural unemployment

Investment displaces labour

One of the main underlying reasons why a macroeconomic recovery will not create enough jobs is structural unemployment. Conventionally this has meant the substitution of capital/investment for labour. This has been happening on a *rising* long-term trend.

Thus, in the 1950s, industrial investment tended to create jobs on a major scale, with the demand-pull for industrial labour offsetting a historic decline in agricultural unemployment and under-employment.

In many industrial sectors since the 'seventies investment has tended to displace jobs. For a while this was offset by continued increase in employment in private and public services. But as budgetary and other pressures have reduced public sector employment, structural unemployment has risen.

The econometric evidence again indicates that reductions in unemployment with recovery are starting from and ending at higher levels in successive cycles.[3]

Disinvestment by small and medium enterprises (SMEs)

This is apart from structural change in the sense of larger market share accruing to bigger business. This was an effect anticipated in the Cecchini report and appears to be happening. Thus small and medium firms, which constitute up to seventy per cent of employment in the Union, are losing market share to larger firms.

Part of the problem is that small and medium firms tend to be local or regional in their production and employment base.

They lack the range of gains open to multinational corporations, which can combine high capital and knowledge intensive production in more developed areas while exploiting low cost labour in other regions of the world economy such as South East Asia for that part of their production sequence which is labour intensive.

As Alexandre Lamfalussy argued thirty years ago, faced with intensified competition many SMEs tend to adopt a defensive investment syndrome rather than innovating new products, new processes of production or new methods of work organisation. As a result, small firms — and especially family firms — may maintain profit rates for some time by not undertaking new investment, and then realise lump sum capital gains by the sale of assets. In other words they disinvest and go out of business.[4]

1.3 Technological unemployment

Added to this are new dimensions to technological un-employment. Again, the conventional definitions assumed that new technology could displace jobs. Computers and other forms of electronic data processing such as switch cards were a classic case in point. For some time it was assumed that new demand generated by new technologies would offset technological unemployment. But it did not necessarily do so for the same people.

Moreover, in a range of private services, there now is a trend to net technological unemployment. This is evident in retail banking in the United Kingdom, and is likely to become more evident elsewhere in the Union.

Overall, private services no longer are offsetting the relative decline of industrial employment, and new technology is playing an asymmetric and probably irreversible role in this process.

The trans-European information networks will both create and destroy jobs. For instance, the leading 'information super-highway' company in the US, Bell Atlantic, has announced 5,600 redundancies over three years because its transition to fibre optics implies job losses in its copper-based communications division.

Further, while smaller firms may have a competitive advantage in flexible use of computers, both in production and services, this is less clear in their access to new computer super-highway information systems, or even available technological advance in the form of patents.

In this sense, the trans-European information networks could prove to be to their disadvantage unless countervailing measures are taken. They need to be backed by reinforced networking between medium-sized firms of the kind analysed later in this chapter.

1.4 The new competition and unemployment

Meanwhile, a new competition is sweeping global markets. This is partly technology based, but mainly concerns the organisation of production and distribution.

A key feature is new flexible or 'lean' production pioneered in Japan, recently applied by many companies in the US, and sometimes also referred to as 'corporate re-engineering'.

Flexible or lean production is as revolutionary as was Henry Ford's introduction of mass production at the beginning of the century. Implying more flexible use of capital equipment and labour, its economies of *scope* can double or treble productivity relative to old style economies of scale.

Flexible production involves the whole chain of suppliers and distributors in an innovation trajectory. It also implies the concept of 'constant improvement' or constantly seeking annual productivity increases.

A report for the Commission shows that through the whole range of mechanical engineering, the most efficient Japanese firm is 1.5 to 3.5 times more productive than the most efficient German company.[5]

In general it is suppliers which are the main casualties of transition to flexible production, with cuts in the number of supplying firms of up to a half or more. Again, as with the expected Cecchini style effects of the internal market, the main losers are small and medium firms.

The potential employment loss for Europe if it does achieve flexible production is illustrated by a US consultancy study which argues that half of the one million people employed in the European auto components sector must lose their jobs if the sector is to become competitive with Japan.[6]

II
THE COMMISSION AND THE EUROPEAN COUNCIL

Both the Commission and the European Council have taken actions over the last two years which have shown a high degree of awareness of the nature of the new methods of flexible production and the need for new financial instruments to support the investment programmes of the White Paper.

But both also have tended to qualify their recommendations or decisions in a manner which risks insufficient action to avoid a further major rise in unemployment.

2.1 Questions on the new European Investment Fund and employment creation

This is well illustrated in the recent history of the proposals for the European Investment Fund.

As made plain in the Commission's first proposal of January 1993,[7] this was conceived as the Union's first instrument of macroeconomic policy with the objectives of:

- countering the cyclical trend to negative growth evident at the Edinburgh Summit;
- making available means to fund not only the trans-European transport and information networks, but also equity investment in small and medium firms;
- doing so by raising money on private financial markets through Union Bonds in a way which was not subject to the borrowing limits on national governments in the Maastricht Treaty.

The Copenhagen European Council meeting in 1993 also extended the areas for expenditures by the Fund to urban regeneration and certain energy projects.

In practice the introduction of the Fund has meant amendment of the Rome Treaty by all twelve national Parliaments. In October 1993 President Mitterrand called for a 100 billion ecu Fund. The Delors White Paper envisages expenditure projects ranging from a lower limit of 150 billion ecu to 550 billion ecu.

The Mitterrand and Delors calls are mutually compatible, because the Fund could finance a share of many national projects which have been postponed because of relative budget constraints.

Making more effective use of the new Fund and Union Bonds

> *However, Union finance ministers have only approved Union Bond borrowing through the European Investment Fund of 8 billion ecu. They have granted that they may increase this as and when necessary. But it is necessary from now if the Fund is to make its anticipated contribution to both investment and employment.*

This is especially the point because of the time lags involved in implementing projects after they have gained financial approval, which typically can run from two to five years.

But it is also important in the wider sense that borrowings from the Fund can reduce national pressures on national budgets and make it more feasible for member states to achieve the borrowing limits necessary for monetary union.

Further, the principle of equity investments in small and medium firms is a crucial means of enabling many of them to survive and flourish against intensified competititive pressures in the 1990s.

In particular, equity investment relieves such firms of the costs of fixed interest borrowing. In practical terms, a minor equity share in many cases would enable small and medium firms to undertake a re-investment or modernisation programme which otherwise would be postponed through reluctance to increase its debt ratio.

Otherwise there are a host of urban regeneration projects throughout Europe which have been postponed on budgetary grounds. There also are a wide range of projects in environmentally safe energy generation which should be promoted.

> *For such reasons a projected 8 billion ecu limit on borrowings by the European Investment Fund gives the wrong message to associations of small and medium firms, and local and regional government.*
>
> *In saying that they will increase this limit as needed, finance ministers are classically reacting to events rather than acting now to change events. With other pressures on national budgets, the result also could be a delay in*

Union funding of trans-European information and transport networks.

2.2 The relevance of new Commission programmes

The Commission has shown considerable perception of the scale and nature of structural unemployment. This is evident within the terms of reference of the 4th Framework Programme which has scheduled funding for research into social exclusion and the rise of a new European underclass.

On the other hand (i) the programme has scheduled only 14 to 21 million ecu for four years research into social exclusion divided between twelve countries; (ii) the original time schedule for the 4th Framework Programme is slipping; (iii) research funds for those involved in the project probably will not be allocated until well into 1995; (iv) the expenditures for the research programmes will run until 1998, and (v) the policy decisions arising from them may not be taken until after delivery of final reports in 1999.

The argument is not that all answers are known now to all questions concerning structural unemployment. But many are, from research underaken over the *past* two to five years by many public policy researchers.

The Committee could be gaining the advice of such researchers within the next year in order to make action recommendations to the Commission and the European Council.

Otherwise, the Committee also could consider the case for (i) scrutinising the initial allocations under the 4th Framework Programme by the Commission; (ii) encouraging the higher rather than lower research budgets on social exclusion of 21 rather than 14 million ecu.

2.3 The White Paper, new technologies and unemployment

Optimism in the White Paper

The Delors White Paper was highly optimistic about the potential job creation from new technologies. There recently has been a reconsideration within the Commission about such job creation potential. It is well warranted.

There is a widespread view that the main impact of the new technologies will be negative for employment overall.

This appears justified in terms of the already available evidence that employment in both industry and services now is tending to go negative under the impact of new technologies.

Alternative strategies for both technology and its dissemination are available, and are not excluded by the Commission. Some of these involve civil applications of defence technology. Others imply alternative applications of the skills of scientists and technologists in the defence and other advanced technology sectors in the civilian field.

Most of these alternative technologies have commercial applications. Others have potential applications in areas of socially useful production.

The committee should consider gaining its own evaluation of both the impact of technological unemployment and alternatives to it. It also should consider the specific new issue of diversification and civil alternatives for the workforce in defence related sectors.

2.4 The new competition, productivity potential and employment

Commission perceptions — public unawareness

The Commission is well aware of the implications of the new competition from flexible or lean production for European competitiveness.

This is especially evident in the *Industrial Technology* and *Information Technology* provisions of the 4th Framework Programme, which stress the importance of the use of new technologies in assisting corporate reorganisation and adaptation of bigger and smaller enterprise to new technologies in the transition to flexible or lean production.

The arguments also carried sufficient conviction for the Commission to recommend and gain acceptance of the European Council for the introduction of the new Objective 4 of the Structural Funds, which explicitly aims to assist management and the workforce in enterprises to adapt to new methods of work organisation.

All of this is positive. It also implies a major paradigm shift from the model of industrial policies as state subsidy of R & D to a range of measures by which the social partners can be encouraged to achieve new methods of work organisation.

The problem is that this *implicit* shift in Commission thinking has not been translated into an *explicit* shift in public perceptions. Only some people in some firms are aware of the implications. Much management in smaller and medium companies seems oblivious.

The need is to translate the revolutionary implications of the efficiency and productivity gains of the new production revolution into social awareness that such gains can generate the resources both to create new employment and finance a major share of the social costs and benefits which are needed if the postwar model of welfare is to survive, in whatever modified form.

Transition to flexible production and 'continuous improvement'

The Japanese, who have pioneered the new production and distribution techniques, talk of them in terms of the *big leap* in transition to economies of scope and the *small steps* of 'continuous improvement' in productivity.

The 'big leap' involves transition from Fordist mass production and economies of scale to post-Fordist economies of scope.

The arguments are well appreciated by German, French and Italian companies who are faced by devastating competition from flexible producers in Japan and the United States.

But transition to flexible production has been implemented already in practice by leading UK firms under the influence of direct relations with Japanese producers or heightened awareness of the implications of the Japanese model.

In this context the Lucas components company in the UK has doubled direct productivity within five years. The Rover company managed to *treble* productivity within two years, from 1981 to 1983. Both companies effectively halved their component suppliers and thus created significant indirect unemployment.

On the other hand, some econometric estimates indicate that if less than a third of European manufacturing industry were able to double productivity through transition to flexible production, this would restore average productivity levels to their highest postwar levels.[8]

Positive and negative implications

The positive aspects of this are that (i) the historic shift to flexible production offers the Union a way to achieve the kind of competitiveness urged in the White Paper; (ii) the major productivity increases would make possible higher earnings for the companies concerned and their employees; (iii) to the degree that profits are raised the volume of corporate tax would increase without an increase in tax rates.

The negative aspect is that the creation of more unemployment through such transition is inevitable.

Further, no estimates as yet appear to have been made of what the unemployment implications of such a transition would be. For instance, they were not taken into account in the low estimates of potential net employment growth cited at the beginning of this chapter.

The resulting prospect is not only that the 15 million jobs target in the White Paper is unlikely to be met but that the net job creation for the Union as a whole for the rest of this decade could be minimal and maybe zero. In other words, new jobs created in areas such as the trans-European networks would be offset by the combination of ongoing unemployment from the trend in structural and technological unemployment plus job losses from the transition to flexible production.

III
GROWTH, DISTRIBUTION AND EMPLOYMENT

The essentials are clear. Recovery is happening but needs to be sustained. Restructuring, and especially the transition to flexible production, is imperative if Europe is to be competitive on world markets. But new dimensions to redistribution of the gains from productivity increases also will be imperative if social cohesion is to be ensured.

3.1 The structural dimension

Economic productivity and an efficient economy

It has already been claimed that the 'big leap' of transition to flexible production in less than a third of European manufacturing could raise productivity levels to levels comparable with those achieved during the period of the so-called 'economic miracles'.

This is imperative if the member economies of the Union are to achieve levels of efficiency comparable to those of leading Japanese firms and those firms in the US which already have achieved comparable levels by learning from and applying the Japanese model.

Such a transition needs to be matched by the process of 'continuous improvement' in efficiency both in assembly firms and their chain of suppliers and distributors similar to that achieved by Japanese leading firms with their first and second tier suppliers.

Insiders and outsiders

The problem is not only that transition to flexible production will cause unemployment as firms going flexible cut the number of their component suppliers. It also lies in the fact that going flexible either creates some unemployment for assembly firms or generates next to no additional employment.

This gives a new structural dimension to the issue of insiders and outsiders: i.e. those already in and those without employment.

The insider-outsider debate in recent years has involved some argument that if trades unions were prepared to accept lower wages, or employers able to cut benefits, more workers would be attracted into employment.

This argument is unproven, at least in bigger business, where productivity gains for some time have been sufficient for management to cover costs and offer real wage increases without significant increase in employment. Nonetheless, the new production flexibility is likely to increase the insider-outsider divide.

Transition to flexible production will tend to strengthen the position of 'insiders' retained by larger assembly firms. Insiders will be paid more for cooperating in the new flexible production methods and techniques, including multi-skilling and an end to many of the specialised craft practices associated with uncustomised mass production.

Inversely, if not offset by other measures to widen the potential gains, transition to flexible production will increase the number of 'outsiders' who lose their jobs as part of the reduction of component suppliers.

There are going to be more outsiders, over all age groups, in the next few years.

Shorter working hours?

If this new dimension to structural unemployment is to be offset, it will mean addressing the question of reduced working hours. This has already been an issue in Germany with companies such as Volkswagen. It also has been part of the political agenda in France.

Some econometric analyses indicate that the macro-economic effects of reducing aggregate working time by 2.5 per cent over five years and by 3.5 per cent over a ten year period could create over nine million jobs. This is nearly two thirds of the 15 million jobs target of the December 1993 White Paper.[9]

The issue of reduced working time is controversial. The question whether the Union should negotiate a policy on it for decision by the European Council certainly would be so.

However, granted the pessimism of the other scenarios for employment creation, and their implications for the European project itself, it is strongly arguable that the Committee should seek evidence on the matter from relevant economists, the social partners, and the Commission.

A key question is viability and implementation. It certainly is not clear that it could be feasible for small and medium firms without affecting their economic viability. On the other hand, it could be feasible if phased over a sufficient time period for workers in both bigger multinational business and in the public sector.

Reduced working hours could be offered in a manner which enhances the rights of people at work to negotiate the manner in which they would choose the hours to be reduced, for instance as hours per week or working days per year.

Importantly, in the productive sector, reduced working hours need not involve reduced pay in bigger business in the degree to which they were able to achieve transition to flexible production and distribution.

Even the productivity gains from Japanese style 'continuous improvement' rather than the quantum leap to flexible production would more than cover the costs concerned.

3.2 The social dimension
Social productivity and an efficient society
Another way of creating employment on a significant scale, and promoting social cohesion, would be to adopt a strategy to increase the number of teachers, health care workers and other carers in the social sphere.

Thus while economic productivity implies more output per worker, and is vital in the productive sphere, *social productivity* would mean a Union policy which consciously aims to reduce class size per pupil, the number of patients per doctor, the number of clients per social worker, etc.

Although the concept of social productivity in this sense is new, the objectives themselves are not. Certainly an efficient society should be judged by the quality of service in the social sphere.

Also, if target levels were negotiated and agreed as Union policy over a transitional period, the costs could be financed not only from sustained economic growth but also from the savings in unemployment benefits.

Again, granted the probability that growth itself is not going to produce enough jobs, the issue deserves examination.

Reducing the underclass and redeploying skills
One of the main aims of a policy for reducing working time or employing more teachers, health workers or carers for the elderly would be to increase recruitment of young people into the workforce and thereby contribute to a reduction of the new underclass of unemployed or under-employed young people.

On the other hand, especially in the productive sphere, reduced working time should not exclude many of those who have been unemployed for the first time in middle life, and are finding it impossible to gain alternative employment at their appropriate skill level.

This obtains both for highly qualified engineers and others facing job losses in the defence and defence related sectors and also for less qualified workers who could be redeployed with retraining.

The strategies for reducing working time and increasing employment in the social sphere certainly could make more sense of the training and retraining programmes of national governments, and within the framework of the Structural Funds.

In turn this could offset the cynicism of many unemployed young people, and also restore expectations among pupils and students that they have a real chance of gaining employment appropriate to their skill levels and qualifications.

There has been a range of areas in which Commissioner Flynn has proposed new employment programmes on such lines. These include:

Local services
- Home help for the elderly and handicapped, health care, meal preparation and housework.
- Minding pre-school-age children and schoolchildren before and after school, including taking them to and from school.
- Assistance to young people facing difficulties, including help with schoolwork, provision of leisure facilities, especially sports, and support for the most disadvantaged.
- Security in housing, and especially apartment blocks in urban areas.
- Local shops kept in business in rural areas, and also in outlying suburban areas.

Quality of life and leisure and cultural facilities
- Renovation of rundown areas and old housing with a view to increasing comfort (such as heat and noise insulation).
- Development of local public transport services, which

should be made more comfortable, more frequent, accessible to the handicapped and safe, and the provision of new services such as shared taxis in rural areas.

Environmental protection
- Maintenance of natural areas and public areas (local waste recycling).
- Water purification and the cleaning-up of polluted areas.
- Monitoring of quality standards.
- Energy-saving equipment, particularly in housing.

The audiovisual sector
There also is employment potential from applying new technologies to distance learning, both in formal education and for those outside the formal sector, including the unemployed.

Such programmes could increasingly include:
- Youth education and training;
- Adult education and retraining;
- Women's education, training and retraining;
- Ethnic minority programmes.

Experience indicates that such programmes need to be combined with local institutional support, which again has employment implications.

A university without frontiers
There also is a strong case for increasing access to higher education for the unemployed, part-time workers or other workers through introduction of a distance learning university of the Union.

Whatever it was called — possibly University Without Frontiers, or University of the European Union, such an institution could build on the positive distance learning experience of the British and Dutch 'open' universities, and up-grade advanced learning and skills for many people who otherwise would not have formal access to higher eduction.

3.3 The spatial dimension
Overall there is considerable evidence that interregional transfers are meeting strong resistance at national level in

some member states such as Italy. At Union level there is also evidence of reduced public support for a single currency in some other countries, especially Germany.

This coincides with new thinking on regional policy which indicates that cash transfers from the centre to periphery of the Union may have promoted or defended some employment levels, but has had limited success in promoting a viable and internationally competitive local economy.

Networking medium-sized firms

Some of the new thinking on regional policy has focused on the concept of networking medium-sized firms and, with them, their smaller component suppliers and sub-contractors.

Essentially, networking aims to give medium firms some of the features of larger multinational companies without them needing to do so by organic internal growth or formal mergers.

One of the key features of networking firms is strategic alliances in specific areas such as joint sales representation in third markets.

Reinforcing entrepreneurship

Such networked medium and smaller firms should be able:

- to represent themselves on foreign markets — or other markets in the Union — as a 'virtual multinational';[10]
- to act *like* a multinational firm in considering the degree to which their own production and distribution networks need to be rationalised;
- to develop new products and processes together;
- to jointly exploit new information technologies and data bases in the context of the new trans-European networks;
- achieve mutual complementarities in cases of diversification from defence related production and
- jointly apply for assistance under the 4th Framework Programme and other Union policies aimed to assist their own transition to flexible production.

Rationalisation of production to raise profitability was one of the main ways in which the Belgian Government in the 1960s and 1970s helped to overcome the 'defensive investment' syndrome noted earlier with reference to Alexandre Lamfalussy.

Analysis of several such companies — which had appealed for state aid — found that some of them were making positive rates of return on a few products, but negative returns on others. Rationalising meant playing to their strengths by specialising in products with positive or potentially positive rates of return, with the result that many companies were turned round to the point at which they did not need external subsidy and could maintain or extend their employment levels.

This case is even stronger within the context of networking, granted that many of the medium sized firms in the Union which are facing declining market shares or lower profits are too often competing against themselves, rather than cooperating in order to compete better against other international competition by rationalising their mutual production and markets, or jointly opening up entirely new markets or products.

Reinforcing Commission policies on networking
Like transition to flexible production, interregional and inter-national networking is essentially an issue of *reorganisation* within new horizons and perspectives. It also is potentially as revolutionary for the medium firms concerned and their smaller sub-contractors and suppliers.

The Commission is aware of such arguments and took them into account in shaping networking policies such as RECITE (Regions and Cities of Europe). It also has introduced networking into some of its cooperation with countries in central and eastern Europe, such as the STRUDER programme for two regions in Poland.

However, the RECITE programme allows for networking over the whole range of local authority activities, and has been criticised with reason on the grounds that it so far has mainly constituted bilateral exchanges of experience.

Also, several other so-called networking programmes of the Commission such as the Atlantic Arc, COTRAO for the Alpes Occidentales, the Euro-District of Saar-Lux-Trier-Westphalz, etc. are of geographically adjacent areas in which the authorities concerned have tended to concentrate on improving mutual infrastructure rather than seeking to assist links between firms.

In general, the potential of the networking concept for medium firms needs to be boosted if it is to help them in the six main areas outlined above and, not least, thereby reinforce their ability to protect and improve employment.

IV
THE STRATEGIC FRAMEWORK

Above all, not least if policies for growth and competitiveness are to improve employment, the strategic framework needs to be coherent and projected with vision.

This does not mean claiming that Commission or Union policies of themselves can affect the vital change from growth *without* jobs to growth *with* jobs.

Especially, it should be evident that some of the possible directions for new policies, such as reduced working time or the new 'social productivity', imply negotiation at local level between social partners in a context which is flexible, specific and related to real needs. Otherwise no general policies in such an area will succeed.

Raising public awareness: a 1992 style programme

Nonetheless, it is vital for the Union to raise public awareness both of the coming new unemployemnt and (i) the positive potential of transition to flexible production for an efficient economy, and (ii) the potential gains for an efficient society from strategies such as work-sharing and socially useful production and services.

This should aim to raise public awareness in the manner of the 1992 internal market programme, while stressing the difference that re-achieving full employment can involve people themselves, at work, currently out of work, in local government decisions, and in local initiatives.

In particular, the Committee should recommend that the scope for transition to flexible production should be reinforced by a special Commission Action Programme which moves the awareness of the issues by some firms into a genral public awareness that Europe can achieve the efficiency gains needed to assure competitiveness and generate resources for social expenditures on job creation.

Part of the unallocated reserve on the 4th Framework Programme could be scheduled for this.

The relevance of Maastricht

The policies also need a framework in which they are not imposed on individual member states. This is despite the fact that they could come within the scope of articles 103.2 of the Treaty of Maastricht, which was stressed at the European Council meeting in Copenhagen by Commission President Jacques Delors.

Article 103.2 establishes that:

The Council shall, acting on a qualified majority on a recommendation from the Commission, *formulate a draft for the broad guidelines of the economic policies of the Member States and of the Community* . . .

The article is important because it concerns the policies of the member states and the new union and not simply the budget of the Commission.

Article 3.a(1) of Maastricht also refers to setting 'common economic objectives'.

Clearly the December 1993 White Paper does constitute a common economic objective and the Committee should take evidence on feasible ways of achieving the fifteen million job target.

Arguably, it also should publish its own recommendations in a form which is relevant not only for the Commission and the European Council, but also debate by the social partners, the Committee of the Regions, and the public at large.[11]

Footnotes

1. Stuart Holland, *The European Imperative: Economic and Social Cohesion in the 1990s*, Spokesman, Nottingham, 1993.
2. Paolo Cecchini, *The European Challenge 1992; The Benefits of a Single Market*, Wildwood House, 1988.
3. Paul Ormerod, *The Death of Economics*, Routledge, London, 1994.
4. Lamfalussy, A., *Investment and Growth in Mature Economies*, Macmillan, London, 1961.
5. Peter Brodner, *Mechanical Engineering*, Report to DG XII. Fast-Monitor

Programme, Commission of the European Communities, Brussels, Sepember 1993.

6. Report to the Commission of the European Communities by the Boston Consulting Group. cit. *Draft Communication from the European Commission of the European Automobile Industry.*

7. *The European Investment Fund (EIF): Proposal for an addition to the protocol on the statute of the European Investment Bank*, Commission of the European Communities, COM(93) 3 final, Brussels 12 January 1993.

8. Stuart Holland, *Big Leap — Small Steps: the implications of transition to Post Fordism for European Productivity, Welfare and Employment*, Associate Research in Economy and Society, London.

9. Stuart Holland, *The European Imperative: Economic and Social Cohesion in the 1990s, op.cit.*

10. Thus a range of separate engineering companies in Catalonia, Tuscany, le Nord, Hesse and the West Midlands may be facing increased difficulty in world markets, but lack the resources to be able to maintain a permanent export representative on the West Coast of America or in South East Asia. Together they could afford to do so. The term 'virtual multinational' was originated by Professor Michael Cooley.

11. The procedures for this as a rolling medium term debate on new options for the economies of the member states and of the Union were elaborated in Chapter 1.2 of Stuart Holland, *The European Imperative, op.cit.*

CHAPTER 3

The Thirteenth State

Ken Coates

On December 1st, 1994, the first report of the Temporary Committee was debated in the European Parliament at the Brussels plenary session. The debate was opened by Ken Coates with the following words.

We are about to celebrate the enlargement of the European Union. But this debate concerns the condition of the present Union, in 1994. This is usually reported to include twelve member states, but in fact there is a thirteenth, the state of Exclusion.

Today we consider how things have been going in the thirteenth state. It is a populous territory. It includes more people than the unemployed, whose condition is our current concern: but those denied work comprise at least eleven per cent of our Union, no less than eighteen million people. Counting them is difficult, but these figures are certainly not exaggerated.

The inhabitants of the thirteenth state often settle there for a long time. Forty-three per cent of those unemployed have been so for a year or more. 7.74 million people are involved. They number more than the citizens of Denmark, Ireland or Luxembourg, more than Finland or Norway, about the same as Austria. Youth unemployment still runs at double the general rate.

How do things go in this thirteenth State? It is not difficult to document rising misery, to pinpoint areas of severe deprivation, to count the victims of child poverty.

I was asked to visit a school in my own Constituency. The headmaster, Richard Rutherford, was appointed this January.

He found that his children could not concentrate on their lessons. They were too hungry.

But misery still elicits a human response. This good teacher organised local people to help, and they began to provide breakfasts for the children as they came into school. Within a fortnight, some of the parents were coming in to breakfast, too.

Distress like this is multiplied by millions in the thirteenth State. But the effort to fight it also enlists large numbers of people. I think of the village of Whaley Thorns, foresaken for sixteen years since the mine closed, surviving on benefits and willpower, half abandoned, with many of the houses closed and boarded up against the world. And I think of the councillor for that village, Mrs Goucher, who has begged the use of a wooden hut, and also begged a clutch of computers on which to teach the young people in the village (and some older ones) how to modernise themselves into whatever labour market there may be.

Fortunately, these people are not entirely alone. Help has been promised, and could be delivered to many, if the resources were made available.

That is why we want the White Paper on Growth, Competitiveness and Employment to be fully implemented. Implementation, however, needs more than agreement in principle. It requires the will to raise the necessary resources. In particular, it requires an agreement to extend the European Investment Fund, or other relevant instruments, to fund all the measures envisaged in the detailed proposals of the White Paper.

Two people have been especially associated with these proposals. Mr Flynn is likely to remain with us, to continue his work for the people of the thirteenth State.

As for President Delors, he could certainly, if he wished, win any election which might be declared in the territories of the thirteenth State. But we are losing him. I hope our Parliament, just like my local voluntary campaigners against exclusion, will salute his departure by overwhelmingly approving this report, and thus ensuring that we continue and fulfil the tasks he has defined.

He understands very well that this project has united differing traditions. Some of us will be voting for it to uphold the values of solidarity. Others would give those values an older name, speaking of Christian Love. And that is why, Mr President, we are asking you to carry a strong message to the Council of Ministers at the Essen Summit. We want you to tell them, in the words of paragraph 40 of our report that

'We cannot afford to fail our peoples in this promise. The states and institutions of our Europe will be measured by their success in facing this challenge.'

PART II

The Essen Summit and the Role of the European Investment Fund in Employment Generation

CHAPTER 4

The Essen
European Council Report

The European Council met in Essen on December 9th and 10th 1994. It acknowledged the fight against unemployment as a 'paramount task', and agreed a five-point programme of action. There follows an excerpt from the Summit Communiqué.

K.C.

The European Union has entered a new phase marked by a number of significant changes. The European Parliament, endowed with additional powers under the Maastricht Treaty, was renewed following the fourth direct elections in June 1994; the new European Commission will shortly begin work; on 1 January 1995 the new member states — Austria, Finland and Sweden — will accede to the Union, and the European Council welcomes them most cordially. With their experience and traditions, the new member states constitute a valuable enrichment for the Union. The European Council trusts that all the remaining preconditions for accession to be put into effect on the scheduled date will be completed in good time.

Following the worldwide recession, our economies are back on track. There must be further determined efforts to improve competitiveness and the employment situation, and to reduce government deficits and create a more efficient public sector. If the economic upturn is to be given further impetus it is essential that, in the European Union too, the results of the GATT Uruguay Round be ratified, and the necessary internal measures for its implementation, including trade-policy instruments, be adopted before the end of the year, so that they can enter into force as planned on 1 January

1995. In this context, the European Council confirms its support for the European candidacy for the post of Director-General of the World Trade Organization, and notes that the developing countries are also supporting this candidature.

The European Council in Essen is the last summit which Jacques Delors will attend as President of the European Commission. His name is associated with what must be the ten most successful years of European unification. He was the prime mover in the Single European Act. He helped the Community realise the visionary goal of the completion of the Internal Market (Europe '92), and in so doing, made a decisive contribution to overcoming the period of stagnation at the beginning of the eighties, and to imparting a new dynamism to the integration process. The second great achievement for which we essentially have Jacques Delors to thank is economic and monetary union, the fundamental groundwork of which was his. For this, as well as for the high standards he has set, the Heads of State and Government meeting in the European Council would like to express their thanks and recognition. His achievements for Europe will not be forgotten. President Delors has rendered outstanding service to European unification.

Looking back over the historic work completed since the Community's beginnings, the Union must now demonstrate its ability also to shape the future in the political and economic interests of its citizens.

In this respect there is no shortage of new challenges before it: in the political sphere the 1996 Union Treaty review conference and future enlargement; in the economic sphere the realisation of economic and monetary union, and a contribution to overcoming employment problems; in the technological sphere, the mastery of information society developments; and lastly, the shaping of internal and external security. The new instruments in the Maastricht Treaty, the Union's greater weight, thanks to the accession of new countries, budgetary means adequate for these goals as a result of the recent decision on own resources, are all significant preconditions for these objectives.

The participants in the European Council held an exchange of views with the President of the European Parliament, Klaus Hansch, on the main topics discussed at the meeting.

The participants in the European Council met the Heads of State and Government, and the Foreign Ministers of the Central and Eastern European countries, which are already associated with the European Union through Europe Agreements, and held an exchange of views with them on the strategy for leading these States towards the European Union.

Against this background the Heads of State and Government discussed the essential issues of the day, and established a set of guidelines for short and medium-term measures in the following four priority areas:

— continuing and strengthening the strategy of the White Paper in order to consolidate growth, improve the competitiveness of the European economy and the quality of the environment in the European Union, and — given the still intolerably high level of unemployment — create more jobs for our citizens;

— ensuring the lasting peace and stability of the European continent and neighbouring regions by preparing for the future accession of the associated countries of Central and Eastern Europe and developing in parallel the special relationship of the Union to its other neighbours, particularly the Mediterranean countries;

— strengthening the Union's action in the area of internal security by providing the necessary legal and operational means for co-operation in justice and home affairs, in particular by concluding the Europol Convention during the French Presidency;

— strengthening the Union's democratic legitimacy, consistent compliance with the subsidiarity principle, and developing the different aspects of European citizenship in order to make the functioning of the institutions more transparent and the advantages of belonging to the Union more obvious to the general public, thus enhancing the Union's acceptability to its citizens.

Economic issues

1. Improvement on the employment situation

The fight against unemployment and equality of opportunity for men and women will continue in the future to remain the paramount tasks of the European Union and its member states. The current economic recovery will help in dealing with these tasks. That recovery is not, however, in itself sufficient to solve the problems of employment and unemployment in Europe. We shall therefore have to make further efforts to solve the structural problems. In this process an important role will be played by dialogue between social partners and politicians, in which everyone concerned will have to assume their responsibilities fully.

The measures to be taken should include the following five key areas:

i. Improving employment opportunities for the labour force by promoting investment in vocational training. To that end, a key role falls to the acquisition of vocational qualifications, particularly by young people. As many people as possible must receive initial and further training, which enables them through life-long learning to adapt to changes brought about by technological progress, in order to reduce the risk of losing their employment.

ii. Increasing the employment-intensiveness of growth, in particular by:

— more flexible organisation of work in a way which fulfils both the wishes of employees and the requirements of competition;

— a wage policy which encourages job-creating investments, and in the present situation requires moderate wage agreements below increases in productivity; and finally, the promotion of initiatives, particularly at regional and local level, that create jobs which take account of new requirements, for example, in the environmental and social-services spheres.

iii. Reducing non-wage labour costs extensively enough to ensure that there is a noticeable effect on decisions concerning the taking on of employees and in particular of unqualified employees. The problem of non-wage labour costs can only be resolved through a joint effort by the economic sector, trade unions and the political sphere.

iv. Improving the effectiveness of labour-market policy: The effectiveness of employment policy must be increased by avoiding practices which are detrimental to readiness to work, and by moving from a passive to an active labour market policy. The individual incentive to continue seeking employment on the general labour market must remain. Particular account must be taken of this when working out income-support measures.

The need for, and efficiency of, the instruments of labour-market policy must be assessed at regular intervals.

v. Improving measures to help groups who are particularly hard hit by unemployment: particular efforts are necessary to help young people, especially school leavers who have virtually no qualifications, by offering them either employment or training.

The fight against long-term unemployment must be a major aspect of labour-market policy. Varying labour-market policy measures are necessary according to the very varied groups and requirements of the long-term unemployed.

Special attention should be paid to the difficult situation of unemployed women and older employees.

The European Council urges the member states to transpose these recommendations in their individual policies into a multiannual programme, having regard to the specific features of their economic and social situation. It requests the Labour and Social Affairs and Economic and Financial Affairs Councils, and the Commission to keep close track of employment trends, monitor the relevant policies of the member states, and report annually to the European Council on further progress on the employment market, starting in December 1995.

The first reports will be used to examine, on the one hand, the effects of tax and support systems on the readiness both to create and to take up jobs and, on the other, the inter-relationship between economic growth and the environment and the consequences this has for economic policy. The European Council notes with interest the information provided by President Delors on changes in the present model of economic growth and economic objectives in relation to the environment and time management.

The European Council also noted the experience of Denmark, Ireland and Portugal in developing a framework at national level and structures and procedures at local level, in order to support an integrated concept for development at local level.

2. Economic and Monetary Union — Economic policy guidelines

Just one year ago, the European Union entered into the second stage of Economic and Monetary Union. The new instruments of the Treaty for strengthening the convergence of our economies are being consistently used in order energetically to advance the European unification process in the economic and monetary fields also. The new procedures have created greater receptivity for a lasting stability policy and strict budget discipline. Already in its second stage, the Treaty is producing its stabilizing effect. The task of this stage — stability-based preparation for economic and monetary union — is being accomplished.

Since the European Council in Corfu, clear success has been achieved in the efforts to achieve reliable convergence. Considerable progress has been made in achieving price and exchange rate stability. In most member states, government budget deficits are also gradually declining. Economic growth in the Community has thus gained dynamism. This development must be used for the further improvement of convergence as the indispensable precondition for transition to the final stage of Economic and Monetary Union. A strict interpretation of the convergence criteria on the basis of the Maastricht Treaty is essential if reliable foundations for trouble-free Economic and Monetary Union are to be laid.

The first priority is to achieve the consolidation goals announced in national convergence programmes. Above all the structural deficits must decline in order to prevent a further increase in the rate of debt. Monetary policy must forestall any new inflationary tendencies in good time. In countries with continuing high inflation rates, greater stabilisation efforts are necessary.

The European Council approves the report submitted by the Ecofin Council on implementation of the broad guidelines of economic policy which have contributed to a more favourable development of the economy.

3. CO_2 / energy tax

The European Council has taken note of the Commission's intention of submitting guidelines to enable every member state to apply a CO_2 / energy tax on the basis of common parameters if it so desires. The Ecofin Council is being instructed to consider appropriate parameters.

4. Trans-European networks in the transport, energy and environment spheres

The European Council welcomes submission of the report from the Group of Personal Representatives. It confirms that the eleven projects decided in Corfu and the three new projects concerning the Nordic member states and Ireland have already been started, or can be started shortly. For the rest, the European Council endorses the most important recommendations of the report of the Christophersen Group.

It welcomes the progress that has been made in selecting major transborder projects, particularly with the countries of Central and Eastern Europe and the Mediterranean basin. The European Council stresses the importance of traffic management systems, particularly in the case of air traffic.

The European Council welcomes the creation of a special window at the European Investment Bank for the financing of trans-European networks. The member states, the Commission and the European Investment Bank will continue to monitor progress made in financing priority projects. It shares the Group's view that the financing requirements for each project must be examined individually.

The European Council is pleased that a start is to be made on priority transport infrastructure projects, particularly rail projects, as from 1995.

The European Council calls upon the Ecofin Council to adopt the necessary decisions, acting on proposals from the Commission, to top up the funds currently available for the trans-European networks.

The European Council emphasizes the Group's finding that obstacles are mainly of a legal and administrative nature, and urges the Commission and the member states to take appropriate measures to overcome these obstacles.

The European Council calls upon the European Parliament and the Council to take the necessary decisions on the guidelines for transport and energy in the near future in order to create a lasting framework for the Union's activity in this area.

5. *Information society*

The European Council emphasizes that the Commission Action Plan 'Europe's way to the information society' and the conclusions of the Ministers for Industry and Telecommunications have set the agenda for the development of an information society. The European Council sees the basic decision on liberalizing the telecommunications infrastructure by 1st January 1998 as a decisive step in establishing information infrastructures for the future. In this connection it stresses the importance of new services and information content, as well as the audiovisual sector in its cultural dimension. In this connection the European Council calls on the Commission to prepare proposals for revision of the Directive on television without frontiers, and for a new MEDIA programme before the next European Council.

The European Council stresses the role of the private sector in building up and financing information infrastructures. It requests member states to establish a suitable environment for such initiatives. International co-operation must be further strengthened, above all in relation to Central and Eastern Europe and the Mediterranean. The European Council calls upon the Commission to make appropriate proposals to that end.

The European Council asks the Ministers for Industry and Telecommunications to ensure co-ordination of further measures. It requests the Council to create rapidly the legal framework conditions — in areas such as market access, data protection and the protection of intellectual property — that are still necessary.

The European Council welcomes the G7 Ministerial

Conference on the global information society to be held in February 1995 in Brussels.

6. *Internal market and competitiveness*

The European Council, in agreement with the Commission report, stresses the importance of the internal market. It is now necessary to achieve uniform and effective application of the internal market rules.

The European Council intends also in the future to pay particular attention to the competitiveness of the European economy, as stated in the Commissions paper. In this connection, it welcomes the Commission's intention of setting up a high-level group which will deal with these matters and submit appropriate reports.

The European Council also notes that the high-level Legislative Administrative Simplification Group ('De-regulation Group') has begun its work. It stresses the need to monitor Community and national law for over-regulation. It requests the Group to submit a report by June 1995.

The European Council welcomes the Council Resolution of 10th October 1994, which is designed in particular to remove legal and bureaucratic obstacles in the way of small and medium-sized enterprises.

The European Council requests the Council and the Commission to continue work on legal provisions concerning biotechnology. The outcome must take full account of the need for health and environmental protection, and the need for European industry to be competitive.

Subsidiarity

The European Council took note of the Commission's first annual report on application of the principle of subsidiarity. The European Council welcomes the Commission's intention of implementing rapidly its 1993 programme for the review of existing Community law. It invites the Commission to submit the proposals still required for this purpose as soon as possible, and no later than June 1995. It asks the Council to discuss the Commission proposals speedily, and in a constructive spirit.

The European Council confirms the great importance of the subsidiarity principle as a guiding principle of the Union as established in the conclusions of the Edinburgh European Council. It calls upon all Community bodies to apply that principle consistently in accordance with those conclusions. In this context the European Council stresses that administrative implementation of Community law must in principle remain the preserve of the member states, without prejudice to the Commission's powers of supervision and control.

CHAPTER 5

After Essen:
Back to the Thirties?

Ken Coates and Stuart Holland

As the Rapporteur of the Temporary Employment Committee of the European Parliament, I was responsible for drafting a report on the need to implement the Delors White Paper in full. I was very impressed by the strong consensus we obtained. My report was adopted by 268 votes to 10, with 30 abstentions. It sent a very clear message to the Essen summit.

Overwhelmingly, Parliament agreed that it was necessary to accept the priority of creating fifteen million new jobs by the end of the century, and to adopt the necessary European instruments to do this. Quite specifically, we insisted that the White Paper should be in large measure funded through the European Investment Fund, or through similar instruments, designed to lever a combination of public and private investment outside the restrictions of the Maastricht criteria.

Unfortunately, the promises in this White Paper are in deep trouble, and this paper seeks to show why.

K.C.

*   *   *

The Essen statement is contradictory. The first sentence states that

> 'The fight against unemployment and for equality of opportunity for men and women will continue to remain the *paramount* tasks of the European Union and its member states.'

But paragraph 3 of the subsequent section on Economic and Monetary Union says that

'The first priority is to achieve the consolidation goals announced in the national convergence programmes. *Above all* the structural deficits must decline in order to prevent a further increase in the rate of debt.'

Paragraph 3 also speaks of the need for 'greater stabilisation efforts'.

To cut structural deficits at national level will restrain growth, income, tax revenue and job creation. To eliminate them without a counterpart Union level expenditure would mean massive deflation. If all member states were to conform with the Maastricht criteria — including gross debt reduction — this would mean expenditure cuts equivalent to a fifth or more of 1994 Union GDP. The effects on employment would be catastrophic.

The limits of own resources

Nor would an increase in own resources solve the dilemma, since they would come from national governments and would need to be financed either through higher taxation — which would be deflationary — or by further borrowing, thereby further prejudicing the Maastricht criteria.

It was to avoid this contradiction — rather than just finance projects — that the original proposal of the European Investment Fund was devised in 1992, thereafter being endorsed by the Edinburgh European Council. Its borrowings through Union Bonds do not count against national borrowing by member states, nor therefore on those states' public sector borrowing requirements. The fund thereby could help achieve the Maastricht convergence criteria while offsetting the deflation which this otherwise implies.

The fund's areas of expenditure agreed at Copenhagen include not only the transport and energy projects endorsed at Essen — for the European Investment Bank — but also information trans-European networks, plus investment in urban regeneration and small and medium enterprises (SMEs). In an urban society and an economy where some seventy per cent of employment is in SMEs, these areas are wide enough to make a significant contribution to fulfilling the fifteen million jobs target of the Delors White Paper.

The Fund clearly is needed. It also has to be a major financial instrument if it is to help achieve the dual targets of national stabilisation and major job creation. If it is to offset the deflationary effect of fulfilling the Maastricht convergence criteria, it will need to be a means by which member states can transfer a major share of their current borrowing and gross debt to Union borrowing.

Such a Fund would be a joint instrument for macro-economic policy as well as targeted areas of expenditure. President Mitterrand clearly grasped this when he called for a fund of 100 billion ecu in October last year. Such a Fund would be sixteen times the new window for project finance proposed at Essen for the European Investment Bank. Unlike the Essen window, it could make a major contribution to fulfilling the commitment to a high level of employment of article 2 of Maastricht.

The instrument does not need to be invented. Member governments already have amended the Rome Treaty in the twelve national parliaments in order to enable the Union to borrow and lend on its own account through the European Investment Fund.

Loss of momentum

So why the loss of momentum? Three main arguments have played a role.

The first is economic, on the lines that the Fund was adopted in 1992, when the Union faced recession, and that a counter-recessionary instrument is no longer needed. But this totally ignores the recession which could occur if the budget and borrowing criteria of Maastricht are substantially implemented, and the depression which would ensue if they were met.

The second argument is financial: that major borrowing by the Union would mean upwards pressure on interest rates. But there would be a counterpart *downwards* pressure on rates to the degree that member states reduced their current and gross borrowing to meet the Maastricht criteria. Also, to the extent that Germany funded the reconstruction of the new Laender through the new Fund (as it already has done through the Edinburgh facility) pressure on the federal budget would be relieved, making possible a lowering of German and European interest rates.

The third argument against the European Investment Fund and Union Bonds is political, and comes from those who claim that the Fund is a federal instrument denying subsidiarity. This is at best misconceived, and at worst misrepresentation. The scale of the Fund and its areas of expenditure are decided by member states themselves through the European Council. The applications (as already evident from the borrowings from the Edinburgh Facility) are made by regional governments, local governments, public or private enterprises and banks. This reinforces rather than reduces subsidiarity.

The issue of the decade

What some governments are failing to address is arguably the main political issue of the decade: that unless member states agree to a major increase in the Fund and Union Bonds they will not be able to meet the Maastricht convergence criteria without causing major unemployment. This would not be stabilisation with spontaneous recovery. It would be unemployment without parallel since the 1930s, destabilising both national governments and the European project itself.

It seems evident that the European Parliament should give this issue real priority in the coming months leading to the Summit in Cannes (in June 1995), in order thereby to resolve the contradiction between the Essen claims of the 'paramount' tasks of the fight against unemployment and inequality and the 'first priority . . . above all' of declining structural deficits.

Members of the European Parliament need to seek support from members of all the national Parliaments, if a serious job creation plan is to be adopted. Too few levers remain in national hands to enable comprehensive programmes of full employment to be successfully implemented. But full employment could be a possibility at the European level, if joint action were undertaken. That prospect provides the most compelling argument for European Union, and failure to realise it will strike the most damaging blow at European democracy, whether at the level of the Union itself, or of its member states.

CHAPTER 6

Exports, Efficiency and Expenditures

Ken Coates and Stuart Holland

DG II recommended two papers to us for our consideration of the medium-term prospects for growth and employment in the Union.[1] This is the text of the paper which I forwarded in reply to the Temporary Committee.

K.C.

Stimulus from a 60 becu Edinburgh Facility

The most interesting paper is the Technical Annex of Scenarios to 2000, produced two years ago, which argued in one of its scenarios that:

'in order to compensate for the delay in economic recovery that an increased wage moderation would imply, *the Edinburgh growth initiative is strengthened to an amount of ECU 30 billion both in 1994 and 1995 (60 billion cumulatively)* in public works of Community interest and related fields'.

As interestingly it argued that:

'Given the low rate of capacity utilisation in those years, *no inflationary pressure should be expected of this package (which) would therefore fully support final demand without adverse effects and would improve the logistic environment for private investment and thus would also improve the growth potential'.*

As a result, on this scenario, growth would average 3.7 per cent from 1997 to 2000 with unemployment falling to 6 per cent.

By contrast, the more recent paper from *The European Economy* supplement (January 1995) makes no recommendations concerning the Edinburgh Facility or the European Investment Fund (EIF) and is remarkably sanguine about mechanisms to reduce unemployment to 6 per cent.

Switch from an expanded EIF to export demand

Instead of a stimulus from an expanded Edinburgh Facility or EIF, DG II now expects deflationary effects of fiscal consolidation and wage restraint to be offset by almost unprecedented export growth.

Table 5 of the paper shows a predicted higher growth of exports for the years 1996 to 2000 than has ever been achieved since the 1960s, and a net balance of exports over imports which was *never* achieved except in the recession years of 1991-95.

Moreover, in the 1960s, *both* home consumption and exports were growing at high rates, whereas DG II now argues for restraint of domestic demand.

There also are some important contradictions here.

Over 70 per cent of the trade of the member states is between themselves. If they each restrain domestic demand — either through the deflationary effects of seeking to meet the Maastricht criteria or by DG II's recommended wage restraint, this will reduce mutual imports and thus mutual exports.

The rest of the world economy

In turn this means that the export increase with the rest of the world has to be greater than at any time since the mid 1970s.

But such export demand cannot be assured. The Pacific Rim economies are booming, but whether China will be able to continue to play its key role in this at its phenomenal recent growth rates is constantly questioned in most of the financial press.

Japan's import capacity is limited. In the US, if the Republican Congress succeeds in its demand for balanced budgets, domestic growth will falter. Even reductions of the

US budget deficit would reduce domestic demand and with it demand for European exports.

The Mexican crisis has shown the fragility of even dynamic intermediate economies in the face of globalised capital flows. It already has had serious repercussions on other economies in Latin America.

Including the dire prospects of the former Soviet Union and high debt in developing countries, the rest of the 1990s could prove to be a period of major instability in foreign markets rather than a springboard for an export boom.

The efficiency gap

DG II stresses competitiveness, but its paper shows no recognition of the efficiency gap between Europe and its leading competitors.

This is the main point of the earlier cited paper for the Commission which shows that across the mechanical engineering sector, *the leading Japanese firm is one and a half to three times more efficient than the most efficient German firm.*

New Asian competition now is coming on stream in key sectors. The broad balance of Europe's trade with the rest of Asia is likely to go *negative not positive* unless we achieve a big leap in productivity by transition to Japanese style flexible production, plus many small steps of continuous improvement.

But this increased competitiveness will imply unemployment because a major part of it comes in the reduction of component suppliers to get the Japanese style first and second tier supplier system.

This is indicated by the Boston Consulting Group's prediction that half of the million jobs in the European auto components sector would need to go to achieve Japanese levels of productivity. There are claims that this analysis is exaggerated. But no counter evidence as yet has been proposed.

Besides, as indicated in earlier submissions to the committee, there is evidence that the Asian economies are achieving Japanese style economies of scope through flexible production with wage costs a tenth or a twentieth those of Europe.

What Europe is facing is less an unprecedented export boom than an unprecedented crisis of competitiveness. None of this is evident from the documents recommended to the temporary committee by DG II.

Foreign direct investment and exports

There also is the new trend in direct foreign investment evident on a major scale for the first time from Germany, and among medium sized firms.

This is another qualitative change which it is not evident that DG II has taken into account. Yet it risks substituting the export of investment and employment for the export of goods.

Net and gross employment creation

DG II assumes that eradication of cyclical and frictional unemployment could halve unemployment levels by the year 2000.

But — apart from the new unemployment from transition to Japanese productivity levels in key sectors — past experience indicates that to increase *net* employment requires much higher *gross* employment creation.

During the years 1985 to 1990 ten million jobs were created in the EU, but this reduced the unemployment rate by only just over a quarter — from 10.8 per cent to 8.3 per cent.

To reduce the rate from today's 11 per cent to 5.5 per cent — on past trends alone — would need the creation of not 15 million but 20 million jobs.

Distribution of productivity gains

The January 1995 paper from the supplement to *The European Economy* refers to the manner in which productivity gains since the industrial revolution have been transferred through society as a whole, first from agriculture to industry and afterwards from agriculture and industry to services.

But it does not show how this will happen. If higher productivity implies higher profits and wages in firms and sectors, the market alone cannot ensure that these are spent in ways which generate new employment.

The paper admits the need for physical investment. But the result of higher productivity may as well be excess savings or export of profits in more physical investment outside the Union, as suggested by the evidence on the new foreign direct investment trend.

The paper refers to reorganised working hours, and thus implicitly reduced annual hours. But while there have been notable cases where this has been done — such as Volkswagen — it has been accompanied by lower pay. If replicated widely this would exert a further depressing effect on recovery.

The composition of employment

Of the 10 million jobs created between 1985 and 1990, 6.5 million went to women and 3.5 million to men. Women's participation in the workforce rose from 43.5 per cent to 48.5 per cent.

This proportion is still below that of Scandinavia and Japan. But it is open to question whether a similar increase in women's participation rates is possible in the current upswing, which would mean less job creation in this cycle than in the last.

The former 10 million increase was almost entirely in services. Employment in manufacturing rose by 1.5 million; in agriculture it fell by 1.8 million, while service employment rose by over 10 million.

DG II's paper from this January admits that its measures will not reach the long-term unemployed, and that this constitutes some 45 per cent of total unemployment or 5 per cent of the active population.

What is going to happen to them granted that the fiscal consolidation will mean reduced national budgets and expenditures unless Union borrowing and expenditures are increased?

The effects of the Maastricht borrowing criteria

DG II's analysis in the January 1995 paper implies that the 'boom and bust' syndrome of the late eighties and early nineties was the result of inflationary pressure, especially from wages. It argues that this can be avoided by 'budget consolidation, stability orientated monetary policies and wage moderation'.

Within this context it clearly is expecting that growth itself will promote consolidation, e.g. by higher tax revenue and reduced unemployment compensation.

But it also claims that:

> 'There is also a large consensus that budget consolidation is needed not only for meeting the Maastricht convergence criteria . . . but also as the best approach for avoiding a new bout of over-heating . . . (and to) open the way for the desired crowding in of investment and increase in capacity'.

The January 1995 paper does not make an explicit argument on the effects of seeking to meet the Maastricht criteria. They are just asserted and then summarised in a three line Table 4 with net government lending averaging minus 2.2 per cent of nominal GDP for the period 1996-2000 and gross debt down to 66.4 per cent (6.4 per cent higher than the Maastricht criterion) at the end of the period.

The January 1995 paper therefore does not give an assessment of the fulfilment of the Maastricht gross debt criteria, while its recommended targets for current lending go beyond the Maastricht terms (aiming for an average Union deficit between 0 and 1 per cent of GDP in the year 2000).

During the period 1996 to 2000 it expects private consumption to increase annually by an average of 2.9 per cent and total fixed investment to increase by 6.9 per cent.

There is no explicit assessment of the deflationary effects on private consumption from fulfilment of the Maastricht criteria for budget deficit and debt reductions over the period. Nor is there any reference to the effect on expectations of these cuts in government expenditure.

The only argument on how an annual rate of investment of nearly 7 per cent would be financed is an observation that in phases of expansion household savings tend to decrease but corporate savings increase.

None of it appears to take account of the fact that reorganisation of production for flexibility on the Japanese model may involve little to no net investment. Thus the Lucas LSF auto components company doubled productivity in the 1980s by reorganising production without any new physical investment in plant or machinery other than desk-top computer terminals.

The earlier DG II paper and the European Investment Fund

The earlier DG II 1993 paper was much clearer on the macroeconomic issue. It argued that public deficits as a percentage of GDP should decrease by an average of −3.3 per cent of GDP over the period 1994-2000, but that public investments as a share of GDP should increase by 2.9 per cent per year.

It also gave an indication of how this circle might be squared in its earlier cited recommendation that Union borrowing and expenditures through the Edinburgh facility should be increased to 60 billion ecu.

Without such an increase in the Edinburgh Facility — or now the European Investment Fund — the financing of the investment gap remains in question.

Recommendations

The inadequacy of the January 1995 paper and its stark contrast with the recommendations on the Edinburgh Facility in the 1993 DG II paper strongly underline the need for the temporary committee to gain an independent assessment of the macroeconomic effects of fulfilling the Maastricht criteria.

Its terms of reference should include:
1. analysis of the trend rate of growth of the Union economy from 1991 through to 1999 or 2000;
2. analysis of the trend rate of growth of annual borrowing in excess of the Maastricht target of 3 per cent over the same period;

3. an estimation of the effects on the trend rate of economic growth of reducing both annual public borrowing and the stock of gross debt over the period to fulfil the Maastricht criteria;
4. explicit evaluation of the multiplier effects of this reduction on: [i] employment; [ii] personal income; [iii] savings; [iv] direct and indirect tax revenue;
5. the degree to which these effects will increase or reduce public borrowing requirements;
6. assessment of the net employment or unemployment implications of these scenarios;
7. evaluation of the scale of increase in export performance needed to halve unemployment in the event of no increase in Union bonds and EIF expenditure;
8. assessment of the probability of such an export increase being achieved in terms of trends in the non-Union international economy;
9. quantification of the scale of increase in borrowing through Union bonds and the EIF needed to offset the deflationary effects of fulfilling the Maastricht financial convergence criteria;
10. assessment of the effects on European interest rates of expanded EIF and Union Bond borrowing compensating for reduction of national borrowing to fulfil the Maastricht criteria.

Footnote

1. European Commission Directorate General for Economic and Financial Affairs, *European Economy, Supplement A, Economic Trends, No.1*, 19 January 1995, and *Technical Annex: Scenarios to 2000*, Extract from *European Economy, No.55*, 1993.

CHAPTER 7

The Wrong Message from Essen

Ken Coates and Stuart Holland

When we were able to digest the results of the meeting of the European Council in December 1994, we concluded that the Council had not taken the Parliament's advice. The following note was circulated in the Temporary Committee at the beginning of 1995. It has also been referred to in discussions outside the Parliament.

K.C.

Committed expenditures by 1999

The fourteen transport projects in Annex I of the Essen Declaration total 91 becu. But the Christophersen Group indicates that only 'about half of the projects should take place by 1999.' An arithmetic half (it may be more or less depending on the sums for half the projects) gives 45.5 becu. The ten energy projects cited in the Essen annex total only 5 becu.

On this basis the total order of magnitude is not likely to be much more than 50 becu over four years or 12.5 becu per year or just over 0.2 per cent of Union GDP in 1994. This is near to the estimation error in any reasonably managed system of national accounts. It is not a macroeconomic programme.

Relation to Maastricht annual budget criteria

The Commission estimates that member states borrowing in 1994 over the 3 per cent GDP annual limit of Maastricht will come to some 150 becu. If this were continued to 1999 this would total 600 becu for the next four years.

If such annual borrowing were to be reduced it would be deflationary. If it is to be offset without deflationary effects this needs a Union financial instrument such as the European Investment Fund.

But even if the 50 becu over four years anticipated from the Essen priority expenditures were financed entirely by a Union instrument such as the EIF, this would only contribute just over 2 per cent per year in offsetting the deflationary effects of meeting the Maastricht annual borrowing targets.

Besides which, the programmes are not to be financed in this way. It is anticipated that the new 'window' to be opened by the EIB to finance the committed projects will amount to 6 becu in total rather than per year, or 0.25 per cent of the needed offset each year.

While a sizeable share will come from financial markets, a significant share clearly will have to come from national governments. This in turn will make it more difficult to achieve the Maastricht criteria.

Relation to Maastricht gross debt criteria

The Maastricht terms are that gross debt must be reduced to 60 per cent or less of annual GDP.

For the Union as a whole this implies reducing total borrowing by 884 becu. Even if the target for this likewise were to be by 1999 rather than 1996, it would mean a direct expenditure contraction of some 220 becu per year.

Even excepting Italy, it would amount to a contraction of some 82 becu per year or over 6 times the annual average for expenditure programmes in the Essen Annex.

Combined effects

Including Italy in the gross debt reduction target would mean reducing borrowing by 884 becu or an average of 221 becu a year. The 12.5 becu of the annualised Essen priority programmes represent only just over one per cent of this.

Adding elimination of the 1994 borrowing excess over 3 per cent from 1995 through to 1999 gives a total deflationary effect of 1,485 becu or nearly a quarter of 1994 Union GDP.[1]

This excludes negative multipliers, i.e. the multiplied contraction of income and expenditure following the first round cuts in fulfilling the Maastricht targets.

What is needed to sophisticate the argument is (i) an analysis of the trend rate of growth of annual borrowing in excess of 3 per cent from, say, 1991, with projections through to 1999; (ii) an estimation of the trend rate of growth on the stock of gross debt over the period; (iii) an evaluation of an annual reduction of both current borrowing and the gross debt over the period; (iv) an evaluaton of the multiplier effects of this on employment, income and direct and indirect tax revenues, plus (v) an estimation of the degree to which this in turn will worsen the underlying debt trend by raising unemployment compensation.

Implications of fulfilling the Maastricht criteria

Arguably the Maastricht criteria are misguided, not least in failing to recognise that in a country such as Italy treasury bonds fulfil the role of savings for retirement in a country with hardly any private pension schemes. If this were taken into account then at least a sizeable share of Italy's gross debt should be discounted.

Such factors probably should be taken into account in the run up to the 1996 inter-governmental conference.

None the less, allowing for the need for sophistication the gross orders of magnitude illustrate that:

● fulfilment of both the annual budget deficits and gross borrowing targets of Maastricht would reverse the current recovery and throw the European economy into a depression comparable to or worse than the early 1930s;
● that the contribution of the new Essen 'window' at just over 12 becu per year is cosmetic. It may be well intended but amounts to project finance rather than a macro-economic financial instrument capable of countering the depressive effects of a serious effort to implement the Maastricht budget and borrowing conditions.

The European Investment Fund

Political realities indicate that either the Maastricht conditions will not be fulfilled by more than a minority of governments, or that their conditions will need to be revised in the run-up to the inter-governmental conference in 1996.

But the macroeconomic realities will not diminish by being ignored. What is needed, in the words of the Christophersen Group's final report, is efforts 'to engineer more imaginative and efficient financing schemes, notably in terms of combining public, including Union, and private resources'.

In fact such information was evident in the devising of the European Investment Fund as a macroeconomic financial instrument which could:

1. issue Union bonds much as the US Treasury issues bonds supplementing those issued by its member states;
2. thereby enable member states to transfer funding of major public expenditure projects to the Union;
3. in turn make more possible a meeting of the budget and borrowing conditions of Maastricht without net deflationary effects inasmuch as Union bonds would not count on the public sector borrowing requirements of member states rather than of the Union;
4. enable member states such as Germany to fund a major share of the special reconstruction costs of the new Laender through the new Union bonds, thereby reducing the strain on the federal deficit and German interest rates, with a potential reduction of interest rates throughout the Union.
5. thereby offset an upwards pressure on interest rates through major borrowings through the EIF to finance new investment expenditures.

What is crucial is not only for the Union to boost the EIF but also for it to be ready to defend the principle that its borrowings — as Union borrowings — do not count against national PSBRs any more than US Treasury bonds count against the borrowings by the States of the Union. There are some indications that the Organisation for Economic Co-operation and Development (OECD) may contest this. Any challenge must be rebutted or some of the main potential gains of the EIF in offsetting national debt burdens will be lost.

The European Investment Bank and national expenditure

The role of the EIF and Union bonds was highlighted in the Delors White Paper on Growth, Competitiveness and Employment of December 1993.

But it has been downgraded in the Essen statement of December 1994, which instead has sought to highlight the role of the European Investment Bank and its new 'window'.

This will offer longer maturities and grace periods on borrowing, refinancing facilities for commercial banks, interest financing during construction projects, and other measures which are useful to borrowers. However:

1. there is an opportunity cost from the new window of the Bank, which it estimates will come to total a third of its lending. What it lends to the Essen priority projects it cannot lend elsewhere;
2. there is a similar opportunity cost for national government financing of a major share of the priority projects, compounded by the double penalty that such expenditures will cost against the budget and borrowing limits of Maastricht;
3. this is compounded by the negative effects on confidence in a sustained recovery as the Union pays lip service to the conditions of Maastricht but offers so little to offset it.

The wrong message

In turn this could affect the viability of the priority projects of Essen inasmuch as the wrong message is being given to would-be investors and entrepreneurs:

1. firms considering bids within the TENs framework which are not included in the Essen priority list will not know whether financing will be available for them over the rest of the decade;
2. the Edinburgh criteria for the EIF included small and medium enterprise and the Copenhagen criteria investment for urban regeneration. But neither SMEs nor regional and local governments now know whether this facillty will be available for them during the rest of the decade;
3. national employers' federations and UNICE will be aware of the contradiction between the declared aims of Maastricht on budgets and borrowing and the miniscule nature of the EIB window. They therefore either (i) will discount the prospects for monetary union, with depressing effects on confidence, or (ii) will tend to

discount the aims of the Delors White Paper and with it the prospects for sustained European recovery;

4. trades unions will discount a better future, with negative consequences for other Union programmes such as Objective 4 of the Structural Funds and ADAPT, which are supposed to encourage cooperation between management and labour in the adoption of new methods of work organisation.

International implications

None of the above has taken into account the fact that the new EIB expenditure projects endorsed at Essen are supposed to include not only member states but also the economies of central and eastern Europe.

1. This means a dilution of the projects and their potential effects on internal expenditure, income and employment within the Union.
2. It leaves the central and eastern European economies with a fraction of the 6 becu increased expenditure by the EIB rather than a Marshall Aid programme.

Meanwhile, none of the imagination called for in the Christophersen working group's final report appears to have been demonstrated in the international sphere.

Japan is facing major difficulties in the current recession but still is sustaining a trade surplus in excess of 100 becu per year.

If there were real imagination it would be to see the role of the European Investment Fund as a European version of the IMF which could attract Japan and other Asian surplus countries to invest in its bonds.

In such a way the EIF could fulfil some of the main aims anticipated in its design, including the offsetting of global trade asymmetries by a counterpart recycling of part of global trade surpluses.

This was one of Keynes' main aims in his original 1943 paper which gave rise to the Bretton Woods Conference the following year.

Fifty years on we do not need another Keynes to see that Europe could contribute to doing the job in a manner which offsets the impending economic crisis and avoids the threat to democratic institutions through intolerance, xenophobia and racism of the kind which spawns on mass unemployment.

Footnote

1. 884 becu of gross debt plus 150 becu annual borrowing in excess of 3 per cent of GDP each year for four years. While the 150 becu annual borrowing might be progressively reduced, the deflationary effect measures the difference for expenditures represented by the loss of 150 becu each year.

CHAPTER 8

The Bank, the Fund and Unemployment

Stuart Holland

In response to the arguments in the preceding chapter, and to a document prepared by the Parliament's services, the European Investment Bank circulated a note seeking to explain their relationship to the European Investment Fund. This raised a number of important questions, which had previously been settled administratively. Stuart Holland prepared the briefing which follows to explain the issues at stake.

K.C.

The European Investment Bank has sent suggested amendments to the working document of the Temporary Committee on 'the role of the European Investment Bank and of the European Investment Fund in relation to job creation'.

The message from the the Bank lies somewhere between Pangloss and Pontius Pilate. It claims in effect that it has been doing the best of all possible jobs, yet at the same time virtually washes its hands on the issue of job creation.

The first point is illustrated by the self-congratulatory amendments suggested by the Bank on the excellent work which it has done and its proposal to delete any reference to contention or criticism of its role.

Otherwise it is disingenuous. In claiming a pro-active role it both gives an unsubstantiated claim that it could not achieve its present level of lending if it were not, and then claims to be increasingly pro-active on the financing of the TENs, for which it was given a *political* remit.

It then remarkably proposes deleting the context in which its actions could be more effective including lower interest rates, entrepreneurship, labour skills, fiscal systems etc —

in other words, the main part of the working document which admits that its role should be complementary and supportive.

Extraneous or essential

The Bank's cover letter argues for this deletion on the grounds that

> 'the addition to the conclusions of matters extraneous to the EIB and the EIF detracts from the thrust of the report while failing to do full justice to the new subjects which are introduced. We therefore suggest confining the conclusions to the subject of the report'.

This is nearer the heart of the matter. The Bank wishes to be seen as a bank and not as an integral part of wider macroeconomic policy, employment creation, and economic and social cohesion.

But the Bank was given the EIF precisely to fulfil this role. This is evident not only from the original proposal of the EIF in the context of cohesion, but also from the text of the Commission's paper drafted within a month of the Edinburgh European Council to establish the EIF.

The opening words of the Commission's paper are 'In the context of promoting economic recovery . . .' It sets the Fund's main objectives as: 'to contribute to the strengthening of the internal market and the furthering of economic and social cohesion'.[1]

Recovery and cohesion also are the key roles ascribed for the Fund in the protocol signed by the heads of state to empower the Bank to set up the Fund.

What are recovery and cohesion if not macroeconomic and social issues of the first importance for the European project? If the Bank already was doing such a good job, why did the Council institute another financial instrument to do it?

The Bank's three main points

All of the three points which the Bank states that it wishes to stress with reference to the triangular relationship of growth-competitiveness-employment are open to challenge.

Point 1: Impact on job creation

The Bank's first point is to claim that: 'the member states have the primary responsibility for measures targeted towards improving the prospects for EU growth and lasting jobs'.

But the proposal for a Council decision on Community membership of the Fund specified that 'a speedy implementation of the EIF will *stimulate* sustained and balanced growth within the Community'. What is this if not the intention to register a net effect on jobs?

Is the Bank unaware that articles 3.a(1) and 103.2 of Maastricht establish that the Council on recommendation from the Commission shall set guidelines for the economic policies of *both* the member states and of the Union and that this is the context in which the Delors White Paper set medium-term employment targets?

We can agree on the error margins of macroeconomic modelling. But the main point for us is not that the net effect of the Bank's investment on employment 'is thought to be positive and not negative'.

The employment committee must be concerned to ensure that the Union has financial instruments which in practice can promote employment on a major scale. Clearly the Bank is not sure that it can, which is a reason why the EIF needs a political decision to increase its power to borrow for investment on a scale which *can* stimulate macroeconomic effects.

Point 2: Alternative roles

The Bank's second point is to claim that its role, enhanced through the Edinburgh Facility, is 'complementary and supportive'.

Clearly the role of the EIF should be complementary and supportive of member state action decided at Union level through the European Council.

But the Bank appears entirely to ignore the import of the Explanatory Memorandum on the functioning of the EIF which explicitly refers to the fact that:

'The existence of the Fund will thus facilitate private infrastructure financing by providing a complement *or alternative* to government guarantees for infrastructure financing.'

Such an alternative role is not to be underestimated in terms of the Maastricht Treaty conditions for financial convergence as a condition for monetary union.

As evident from the Commission's own figuring, the convergence criteria cannot be met without taking out the equivalent of a quarter of 1994 GDP from member states current deficits and stock of borrowing unless alternatives through expansion of Union borrowing through Union bonds and the EIF are fulfilled. The Bank is silent on such an essential issue for the committee, for the Parliment and for the unemployed.

Point 3. Financing for SMEs

The Bank claims that the only measure concerned with job creation is the facility for SMEs.

This ignores the central issue of the contradiction between the financial convergence criteria of Maastricht and the political issue of the 'paramount tasks' as stated at Essen of the fight against unemployment and for equality of opportunity.

But it also is not clear that the Bank is aware that the Commission statement on 'The Impact Proposal on Business' of the creation of the EIF refers not only to SMEs but also states that:

> 'the implementation of the TENs will generate a very substantial investment effort (public works, high-tech and research etc) and will therefore result in the creation of an important number of jobs, both for the execution of the investment programmes and for the operation and maintenance of the networks.'

By contrast the same text states of SMEs only that:

> 'financing support for SMEs, especially in Community assisted areas, will help these firms to prosper and develop.'

It may well be argued that support for SMEs also will create jobs. But the Bank's claims to the committee fail to refer to the terms of reference from the Commission for the EIF which, by contrast, stresses job creation through the TENs.

Has the EIB taken a collective decision to ignore the Commission's terms of reference? If it is clear that the TENs will not create 'an important number of jobs', should this not be brought into the open in a manner which enables the committee and the parliament to address how the EIF could do so by other areas of borrowing for on-lending and investment?

Macro insignificance

The Bank advises us with some satisfaction that it has lending of 20 billion ecu. This compares with a Commission estimate of this year's current account borrowing over the Maastricht limits of 150 billion ecu.

If continued for four years to the later target for a single currency in 1999 this would represent a cumulative current account deficit of member states — over and above the Maastricht limits — of 600 billion ecu for the next four years.

Added to this is the stock of member state debt over and above the Maastricht criteria totalling some 884 billion ecu. Summing the two does not need a Nobel prize in economics. It totals nearly 1,500 becu. Even assuming unrealistically that member states from now reduce their current deficits to the Maastricht limit gives an excess over the budget and borrowing limits of Maastricht of over 1,000 billion ecu.

The standing of the EIF

At the moment the EIF is a subsidiary instrument within the Bank. This is not simply a formal matter. It is reflected in the Bank's own attitude.

Whether the Fund can be a major macroeconomic player may prove to depend on whether it stays in the EIB or becomes independent of it.

We should not be distracted by this issue. The important thing about the Bank and the Fund from now is to ensure that the resources of the Fund within the Bank are expanded substantially. Whether the EIF should be detached from the EIB is an issue which nonetheless probably should be recommended in the preparation of the IGC.

In particular, granted the scale of the deflation implied by meeting the Maastricht financial criteria, we need to take seriously the statement in the Commission's Explanatory Memorandum on the EIF that its funding should provide 'a complement or *alternative*' to national government financing.

This point was made by the Commission in the context of infrastructure. But it needs to be extended to other areas in which the European Council already has recommended EIF borrowing and expenditure, such as urban renewal. It relates to the argument that member states will need to transfer a major part of their borrowing to Union bonds if they are to be able to fulfil the Maastricht criteria without further deepening mass unemployment.

References

1. COM(93) final, *The European Investment Fund (EIF)*, Brussels 12 January 1993, mimeo.

PART III

The Preparation of the Final Report of the Temporary Committee

CHAPTER 9

The Feasibility of Full Employment

Ken Coates and Stuart Holland

Early in January 1995, following the Council's Essen decisions, Ken Coates submitted these thoughts on the further work of the Temporary Employment Committee, in preparation for the Final Report, due by July 1995.

K.C.

This paper is not a statement of all that we should be considering or doing, but an attempt to respond to the views expressed in the Temporary Committee during its meeting of January 24th on the strategic areas in which we should be taking evidence, gaining advice and mobilising our case.

1. The macroeconomic context

The key issue now, really, is the contradiction within the Essen statement between making the fight against unemployment 'paramount', while giving 'first priority above all' to reducing member states structural deficits.

Something has to give — either the budget and borrowing conditions in Maastricht, or employment. It is not at all widely recognised how draconian the scale of deflation would need to be to meet the Maastricht targets. This was the point of my paper, 'Back to the Thirties?'.

What is really paramount is the expansion of Union financial instruments which do not count on member states' national borrowing. Only in this way can the Union both reduce national structural deficits and increase expenditures to create employment.

We need to know more on this central issue. This is why I trust that we shall be able to commission an independent study of the employment effects of reducing member states deficits to the Maastricht criteria; the kind of scale on which Union financial instruments would need to be expanded, both to defend existing employment, and make a significant contribution to fulfilling the 15 million jobs target of the White Paper on Growth, Competitiveness and Employment.

We need such a study to gain independence in our own judgements and to be able to better assess whatever evidence DGII may be able to give us of its own assessment.

Reinforcing the Maastricht targets

We also really should be engaging in debate with the Council on this matter. Many finance ministers do not seem to accept that Union borrowing need not compete with their national borrowing, but could help meet the Maastricht financial targets. There also is the so-called crowding-out debate, where some finance ministers again have not registered appreciation that expanded Union borrowing can help them lower national interest rates by lowering national debt.

The White Paper opened this argument at Union level. But there also is some space at national level in at least some member states. In October 1993, President Mitterrand followed the call of Michel Rocard for 50 billion ecu of Union borrowing by saying that it was so excellent a proposal that it should be doubled to 100 billion ecu. Prime Minister Balladur then was asked whether he supported the Mitterrand call, and said that he did.

The Italian, Belgian and Greek governments surely have a vested interest, since they otherwise cannot hope to be candidates for monetary union within the decade.

The German government appears sceptical. But it is not clear to what degree those responsible have appreciated that increasing Union borrowing to finance reconstruction of the new Laender can take the pressure off the federal budget, rather than compete with it.

We feel strongly that this is a legitimate Union issue to be addressed by the parliament within the framework of subsidiarity. For instance, the consequences of taking pressure off the budget of Germany would be a lowering of interest rates throughout the Union, to the benefit of governments, employers — especially SMEs — and citizens of the Union, both directly through lowering borrowing costs, and indirectly through restraining inflationary pressure and creating employment.

Most of the above implies really building and boosting the European Investment Fund as a regional version of what was anticipated at global level for the International Monetary Fund: an instrument which, in Keynes' own terms, should be 'a means of assurance to the troubled world, by which any country whose own affairs are conducted with due prudence is relieved of anxieties which are not of its own making'.

Macro and micro roles: the EIF and the EIB

It means grasping the potential for the EIF as a macro instrument with its agenda set by political decisions at European Council level, as opposed to the micro project-based finance facility of the European Investment Bank which, before the Edinburgh facility, responded only to applications from potential borrowers rather than fulfilling a macro agenda.

I submit that specifying this distinction is a major issue for the committee. Even the Essen agenda means doubling the commitments of the European Investment Bank. Fulfilling the call of President Mitterrand would mean multiplying this by ten. Fulfilling the Maastricht criteria by shifting national borrowing to Union borrowing could increase it by a hundredfold.

The EIB should not be called upon to fulfil this macro role. The European Investment Fund arguably should be separated from management by the EIB and constituted as a separate financial institution.

In this context we should not neglect the potential of the European Union as a relatively new institution. Neither the United States nor Japan can invent a new financial instrument equivalent to European Union bonds of the kind proposed — with expansion of the EIF — in the Delors White Paper on Growth, Competitiveness and Employment.

Until the creation of the Edinburgh facility, the public sector borrowing requirement of the European Union was zero, while the US Treasury borrowing requirement was over-stretched, and that of Japan under pressure.

Shifting national borrowing to the EIF to fulfil the Maastricht targets is technically feasible because the institution already exists, following national parliament amendments of the Rome Treaty to enable the Union to borrow and spend on its own account. We should be highlighting this potential in the remaining term of our remit. We now have the instrument. We should press the Council to use it.

2. Reducing working time — increasing employment

Although controversial, the issue of reducing working time is central to our agenda. With net economic growth and for most levels of activity, fewer hours mean more jobs.

Not least, for various reasons stressed in earlier papers and in the resolution of the Parliament, growth alone may only create a third of the 15 million jobs in the Delors White Paper, and a quarter of the Flynn jobs target.

Table 1
Alternative Macroeconomic Scenarios 1993-1997

	GNP growth 1993-97 (% pa)	Job gains by 1997 (millions)			Reduced Unemployment by 1997 (per cent of labour force)		
	EC	Obj.1	Rest	EC	Obj.1	Rest	EC
Lower Scenario	2.9	0.4	0.8	1.2	0.7	0.3	0.4
Low+>hours	2.9	1.1	2.6	3.7	1.7	1.3	1.4
Low+>hours+recovery	3.4	1.5	3.9	5.4	2.3	1.9	2.0
Higher Scenario	3.1	0.8	1.3	2.1	1.2	0.6	0.8
High+>hours	3.1	1.4	3.2	4.6	2.3	1.6	1.7
High+>hours+recovery	3.5	1.9	4.5	6.4	3.0	2.2	2.4

The assumptions underlying the alternative scenarios for 1993-97 are as follows:
● The **Lower Scenario** implies a Delors 2 increase in the Community Budget or expenditures financed by the European Investment Fund [EIF] equal to 0.19% of Community GNP by 1997.
● The **Higher Scenario** has further increases in the Community Budget or EIF expenditures amounting to 0.25% of Community GNP by 1997 (i.e. a total increase of 0.44% GNP).
● **>Hours** assumes 2.5% reduction in annual hours averaged over all employed persons.
● **Recovery** assumes both fiscal stimulus and expenditures financed by the EIF, resulting in a total accumulated debt equal to 2% of GNP by end-1997.

Table 2
Alternative Macroeconomic Scenarios 1997-2002

	GNP growth 1998-2002 (% pa)	Job gains by 2002 (millions)			Reduced Unemployment by 2002 (per cent of labour force)		
	EC	Obj.1	Rest	EC	Obj.1	Rest	EC
Lower Scenario	2.7	1.5	2.5	4.0	2.4	1.2	1.5
Low+>hours	2.7	2.5	5.3	7.8	3.9	2.6	2.9
Low+>hours+struct.policies	2.8	4.0	10.3	14.3	6.3	5.0	5.3
Higher Scenario	2.8	2.2	3.3	5.5	3.4	1.6	2.1
High+>hours	2.8	3.2	6.2	9.4	5.0	3.0	3.5
High+>hours+struct.policies	2.9	4.7	11.2	15.9	7.4	5.5	5.9

The assumptions underlying the alternative scenarios for 1997-2002 are as follows:
● The **Lower Scenario** implies that expenditures financed either by the European Investment Fund [EIF] or the Community Budget rising from the Delors 2 limit of 0.19% of Community GNP in 1997 to 0.44% of GNP by 2002.
● The **Higher Scenario** has expenditures from the Community Budget or via the EIF amounting to 0.44% of Community GNP by 1997 and 0.60% of GNP by 2002.
● **>Hours** assumes a reduction in annual hours averaged over all employed persons reaching 2.5% by 1997 and 3.5% by 2002.
● **Recovery** should by and large be sustainable by 1997 through a combination of fiscal stimulus and expenditures backed by the EIF, so that EIF borrowing could be held constant thereafter.
● **Structural Policy Effects** assume both policies pursued by member states and the role of the Structural and Cohesion Funds.

In their work for the Holland report on economic and social cohesion for President Delors, the Alphametrics team found that even an average Union GDP growth rate of 3 per cent over ten years would create only 5.5 million jobs, whereas reducing annual working time by 2.5 per cent within five years and raising this to 3.5 per cent within ten years would create 9.4 million jobs (see Tables 1 and 2).

The issue of reducing working time was seriously considered by the Commission in the initial drafts of the White Paper. It then was dropped before the final draft.

Why was the issue dropped? One reason, undoubtedly, was the lack of a high profile debate and discussion on the issue. It was alive in France at national level, and real at company level in Germany. It could be assumed that DG V supported reducing working time. Who opposed it? Should we not be taking evidence from DG II on this?

Table 3
Lucas LSF: The Transition to Flexible Production 1983-89

Key Factor	Change
Labour Productivity	
– Units per Worker	<Doubled
– Value	<Doubled
Product Diversity*	Doubled
Reduction in Factory Area*	20 per cent
Direct Employees	Increased by 10 per cent
Indirect Employees	Reduced from 41 to 14 per cent
Stock Savings*	Average 14 per cent per year for four years
Product Lead Time*	From 21 to 4 weeks

*1982-87.
Source: R. Kaplinsky, *From Mass Production to Flexible Specialisation: Micro-level Restructuring in a British Engineering Firm*, April 1991.

Who gains and who pays?

Of course, there are a range of major problems in reductions of working time. One of the most obvious is who pays, in what way? This relates to another key issue for the committee, which is the degree to which at least leading enterprise can achieve the doubling or trebling of productivity by transition to flexible production, as evidenced by Lucas LSF and Rover in the United Kingdom (see Tables 3 and 4).

There are estimates which were made available to the Delors Forward Studies Unit before the White Paper that, if

Table 4
Rover Cowley Plant: The Transition to Flexible Production, 1991-93

Key Factors	1991	1993
Site Area (acres)	222	114
Factory Area (acres)	104	52
Employees	3550	3300
Vehicles per year	55000	82300
Car per Man per Year	10.9	30.6
Suppliers	410	370
Direct Material	£266m	£554m

Source: R. Kaplinsky, Direct enquiry for Associate Research in Economy and Society, October 1993.

Table 5
Potential Productivity increases, 1994-1998

	Scenario 1		Scenario 2		Scenario 3	
Proportion manufacturing	*10%*		*20%*		*30%*	
affected	*300%*		*200%*		*100%*	
Increase over period						
Results	*Total*	*Annual*	*Total*	*Annual*	*Total*	*Annual*
	%	*%*	*%*	*%*	*%*	*%*
Growth — total	18.90	3.50	21.20	3.90	18.20	3.40
Growth — manufacturing	42.20	7.30	51.10	8.60	39.60	6.90
Growth — other	10.20	1.96	10.20	1.96	10.20	1.96

All scenarios assume:
   productivity gains in fast growth sectors are incremental over the period
   productivity in remaining sectors grows at same rate as before
Standard factors:
   Manufacturing share of total   27.20%
   Normal growth — total   2.14%
   Normal growth — manufacturing   2.62%
   Normal growth — other   1.96%
Source: Alphametrics, Cambridge.

less than a third of Union manufacturing were to double productivity over five years, this would restore average manufacturing productivity to nearly 7 per cent, equivalent to the highest postwar levels (see Table 5).

What this would mean is that many firms could afford to reduce working time while not reducing pay, or actually increasing it.

There are other issues which so far have made reduced working time controversial, including (i) persuading the unpersuaded, and (ii) the fact that many smaller firms could not afford it, and (iii) that different member states, companies, trade unions and individuals might wish to do it in different ways.

On the first point, it is vital to promote debate, not least through the Social Dialogue, but also within and by the Parliament, rather than simply recommend a Commission Directive.

The second point could be met if it were anticipated that the provisions only would apply to bigger business employing more than 500 people (including multinational companies with a total global employment of more than 500) plus the public sector administration.

Reinforcing choice and rights

The third point is a potential strength rather than a weakness. If, after debate and dialogue, the Commission were to draft a directive that average annual hours should be reduced by 'x' within one or two years, why should not the widest range of choice be open on how to do it?

One of the things about the 1992 programme and proposals for monetary union is that most citizens of the Union cannot see how they gain from it. They see them as decisions which do not affect them or improve their daily lives. If, by contrast, we showed that people could negotiate what hours they worked, it could dramatically affect their working and non-working lives. The principle of reduced hours also could still leave companies flexibility for meeting deadlines in the short term.

For instance, a single person without children might be prepared to work overtime, provided that this increased his or her vacation time, or increased time for retraining or re-education. By contrast, someone with children or elderly parents could submit that they should not work overtime except under exceptional circumstances, for which they would be compensated by financial allowances to engage carers.

In this way the issue of reducing average working time could reinforce rights of citizens within the Union in a manner which, in turn, would reinforce the legitimacy of the Union itself.

3. Economic and social efficiency

The committee needs to be seen to be convinced of the imperative of achieving an efficient economy, able to sustain its place at the global innovation frontier. On the other hand, in terms of employment, we should be advocating both an efficient economy and an efficient society.

In the economic sphere, greater efficiency means higher productivity, better quality, greater reliability and the capacity to sustain process and product innovation.

Much of this can be achieved by the 'big leap' of transition to flexible production of the kind pioneered by the Japanese, and replicated successfully by many US and some European companies. This needs to be matched by the many 'small steps' of continuous improvement, or what the Japanese call *kaisen*.

The result is higher productivity in the classic sense of more output per worker. It is inescapable that this will tend to lower employment or the rate of growth of jobs by lowering the employee-output ratio.

This causes problems in itself. But in any event, it is not at all clear that this benchmark for the productive sphere also should apply to the social sphere. Rather, in education, health and social services, the Union arguably should be seeking to raise the employee-client ratio.

Examples are evident and widespread. Ideally, every parent, every teacher and every government would like to reduce the average size of classes in schools, the number of students per lecturer in higher education, the number of patients per doctor or health worker, and the number of clients per social worker.

The Union and an efficient society

The reasons why governments have not followed this agenda in the social sphere are self-evident. They have been concerned about the financial constraints on budgets, as well as the reaction of foreign exchange markets to the worsened trade balances implied by unilaterally increasing public expenditure without a corresponding increase in economic efficiency and exports.

This surely is where we should be able to act as a Union to set an agenda for not only a single currency and increased competitiveness, but also for social efficiency.

Well over 70 per cent of the trade of the enlarged Union is with itself. With even partial transition to flexible economies of scope rather than inflexible economies of scale, leading firms in the Union should be able to achieve major gains in economic efficiency. In this sense, the new Objective IV of the Structural Funds and the ADAPT programme were well conceived, and should be supported. Likewise, the provisions of the Fourth Framework Programme should enable many firms in the Union to stay on, or advance the global innovation frontier.

A single currency would massively reduce the scope for speculation on foreign exchange markets. It would largely restore the debate on what is spent, when, how and by whom to elected representatives. It would mean that Europe could make choices about distribution of expenditure and jobs — as through shorter working hours — without the penalties which now compromise individual member states.

Nor does economic efficiency mean that each and every worker in the productive sector has to work as efficiently as the most efficient competitor in the world economy. Only some 15 per cent of the Japanese economy is hyper efficient in the manner which has been pounding European competition. The rest of the Japanese economy is inefficient to hyper-inefficient.

Yet this strategy makes sense both at the macro level inasmuch as Japanese unemployment is only some 2 per cent, and in the micro sense that limits on the expansion of hyper-markets has meant the survival of employment intensive small local stores and shops, which in turn keep neighbourhoods alive, reduce crime and mean that elderly people without transport can meet their daily needs.

The most recent Japanese economic plan has focused on areas of social expenditure to raise what I have called 'social efficiency'. For instance, it provides programmes for increasing the use of schools for adult education; providing new nursing homes for the elderly; ensuring that children have access to a park within 250 metres of their home; advanced public land purchasing for new housing; up-grading the quality of below standard housing, etc.

Some of this may be overtaken by the need to strengthen housing and public buildings following the tragedy of the recent earthquake. But the twin lessons from Japan of combining economic and social efficiency should not be lost on us. It is how they combine hyper-competitiveness with economic and social cohesion.

4. Reorganisation and new efficiency in the social sphere

While, in the above sense, social productivity is the inverse of economic productivity, social efficiency can not only increase employment, but also improve the quality of the service.

Both factors are vital to the case. An efficient society is one which would reduce unemployment by creating jobs in the social sector. But it also would commit management and workers to better use of fixed plant and equipment and continuous improvement in the social sphere.

The feasibility of doing this has been illustrated by an important study from DG V of the Commission of the Karolinska hospital in Sweden which, by applying the Japanese model of customised flexible production to its services — focused on client needs, increased utilisation of operating theatres by 30 per cent, and reduced waiting time for operations by up to three quarters. Staff were redeployed rather than unemployed. Direct total costs were reduced by 20 per cent.[1]

The implications are potentially dramatic that, in most OECD countries, hospital costs amount to half of total health expenditure.

If replicated throughout the European Union, the savings from achieving better hospital service would be equivalent to 1 per cent of GDP. In turn, this would release resources for more labour intensive services elsewhere in the health sector, or other areas of the social sphere.

Clearly, such reorganisation in the social sphere is not easy. It is a social process rather than a prescription. In the Karolinska case, it met with considerable resistance from professional and other staff before the gains were achieved. Again, the social partners should be involved.

Nonetheless, we should be pushing these concepts and their feasibility through Union action onto the agenda of the IGC and the mid 1990s.

5. Venture finance for small and medium enterprise

SMEs constitute 70 per cent of employment outside the public sector in the Union. They are being penalised massively by conventional bank lending and the unreadiness of European equity markets to match the 'venture capital' typical of the US and the special assistance programmes for SMEs commonplace in Japan.

Venture capital means underwriting risk. Some win and some lose. But a call for more venture capital alone in Europe is not necessarily salvation for many SMEs. The gains from venture capital can be massive, but the costs of dependence on it for innovating small entrepreneurs fatal.

This is not a question of whether firms fail. Success itself can mean the demise of the independent entrepreneur. Studies of the venture capital market in the US in the case of Silicon Valley show that typically new finance in the form of equity holdings assists the growth of small enterprise, but that the venture capitalist then insists on takeover by a larger concern to ensure effective marketing. The original entrepreneur or entrepreneurs then lose control.

In Europe, case after case shows that national and regional banks tend to adopt an outdated approach to innovating SMEs. One example from an Italian firm with less than 500 employees makes the point. The firm had devised new machinery for soft paper manufacture which was several times more efficient than the prevailing competition. It approached national and regional banks with the claim that it could gain up to half the market for such machinery in Japan and Latin America. No bank would offer it any finance for such a venture which was not mortgaged against the corporate and personal property of the entrepreneur.

The firm was highly successful, and went it alone on its own resources from cash flow. It succeeded in gaining 45 per cent of the Japanese domestic market for such machinery, and 100 per cent of the market in Latin America. But this was a high risk strategy which, if it failed, could have meant the failure of the enterprise itself.

Many SMEs with viable products are not penetrating foreign markets because they cannot finance such ventures on their own resources, and are getting next to no assistance from traditional banks or classic financial intermediaries.

Equity holdings by the EIF

One of the main provisions of the European Investment Fund is that it should be able to take equity stakes in SMEs. This is not a matter of the European Union gaining control of companies. It means that investment projects, which could be equivalent to a fifth of the value of the company, are financed by the Union when finance otherwise would not be available except on punitive terms.

The proposal for equity finance for SMEs through the European Investment Fund is excellent. One problem is that it is only scheduled to start operation two years from now. Another is that the scale of expenditures under the Fund are so small that its operations will not be able to register a significant macroeconomic effect from such lending to micro enterprise.

We should make this a major issue in our discussions, debates and proposals. Not least, we need to ensure that there are effective financial intermediaries between the EIF and individual SMEs. Some of the national and regional credit institutions in Italy already are fulfilling this function within the remit of the funds available under the Edinburgh Facility.

6. Training and retraining

It is commonplace in any declaration on employment to highlight the need for training and retraining. But we face real problems in this sphere.

One of the commonplaces of the new reasoning on transition to flexible production is that the training and retraining concerned has to be on the job. In other words, general training and education may be a necessary condition for numeracy, literacy, computer literacy, skills and adaptability. But the key training of value to companies managing the transition to new methods of production and work organisation is specific rather than general, gained in the enterprise, and on the job.

This is well illustrated by the dramatic case of FIAT's new plant at Melfi, where the recruitment policy favoured workers with no previous industrial experience whatever. The result of such has been that virtually all the employees are under thirty years of age. The example is paralleled by several recent direct investments in central Europe.

This has major implications for the training policies of the Union. What it implies is that the time honoured practices of craft training no longer are relevant to the multi-tasked and multi-skilled demands of in-house training for flexible production.

That is why and where we need to consider both economic and social productivity. There are many services in the community where retraining, and in some cases, basic training, could deliver both new jobs and improved social services.

For instance, if we take seriously the case of increasing care and facilities for the elderly, there is no reason why a poor secondary school graduate with low numeracy and literacy skills should not be able to qualify in caring skills.

This is not to devalue social care, but simply to state that caring for the elderly involves practical and human skills rather than academic competence. It may mean taking children to and from school; it may mean child care group leaders to supervise and assist physical activity such as football, basketball or gym activities after school. It may mean helping physically handicapped people. It may mean shopping — or help with shopping for those who are unable to go out by themselves.

All of this is compatible with the recommendations already made in the Flynn White Paper. It also has implications for job creation within the concept of labour intensive social efficiency. It has significance for the carers, as well as the cared for. It implies that many of the high school low-performers, currently stigmatised as drop-outs, can see a role for themselves which is socially useful and professionally paid, increasing their self-esteem and that of those in their immediate environment, not least their families.

7. Innovation agreements

We should be able to find a way to relate the case for social efficiency to economic efficiency at the front line company level. I submit that one of the ways to achieve this may be through the concept of Innovation Agreements. If major productivity gains are feasible by transition from old style economies of scale to new style economies of scope, the question of who gains in what way is crucial.

To its credit, the Commission has made major advances in this regard through programmes such as those of the new

Objective IV of the Structural Funds and ADAPT. The problem is the lack of an institutional means by which the social partners can find Union support for what they increasingly wish to do spontaneously at company level.

For instance, case by case in both Europe and the US, management and unions are coming to realise that the confrontation implicit in the old style Fordist mass production paradigm is inhibiting mutual co-operation to their mutual benefit. Thus, under Fordism, management controlled the speed of the production line, and workers had to adapt. Trades unions did so by trying to slow down the line.

Under post-Fordism or flexible production, management is allowing the workers to stop the line if a faulty product is going through — the so-called *andon* light system in Japan and Japanese transplants. Increasingly it is treating labour as a fixed asset and capital equipment as a disposable asset.

Beyond this, the work ethic is changing. Whereas management previously disposed and imposed, it is increasingly seeking to empower workers with their own choices in work groups of task forces in the context of total quality control. The dramatic result has been that the category of 'worker empowerment' has been the top finding among management objectives in a recent analysis of some 350 companies in the Union.

All this means changing the name of the game in industrial relations. At Union level we should not allow this to go by default. We should be addressing the issue of whether the Union can shape policies which facilitate such increased co-operation between management and labour. For instance, this might mean fiscal incentives to companies to reach Innovation Agreements of a kind which promote co-operation in process innovations and the re-organisation of work. Such incentives would not lower the tax take in companies which can achieve the 'big leap' transition to flexible production by re-organisation of work methods and the greater employee involvement.

Not least, in strategic terms, we should be encouraging management in bigger business to consider labour as a fixed resource, and investment as a variable, as the Japanese do, rather than the conventional wisdom that labour is the variable cost — to be made redundant during recession — and capital investment the fixed cost to be valorised by cutting wages or employment.

Management in several leading European companies already is giving its workforce a commitment to no voluntary redundancies. This is not 'lifetime employment' to the age of 55 as in Japan. But it is a commitment to employment for the lifetime of the company or its particular project. This is especially important in gaining employee support for the productivity gains through continuous improvement or total quality control which otherwise could improve them out of a job.

Little of this is traditional. Most of it means re-thinking conventions on the work process. But we should be considering such issues as part of the re-casting of the agenda for employment at Union level in the post-Fordist era.

8. Accounting and accountability

Information on structural change in industry and services is very limited. Eurostat is dependent on private market surveys or industry publications for much of its data, which then cannot be properly integrated into its own accounting framework.

Virtually no systematic analysis at present is possible of the likely unemployment effects which will follow from more European firms making the 'big leap' transition to flexible production and the reduction of their suppliers.

Examples such as that of the Boston Consulting Group predicting the loss of half of the million jobs may, or may not, be exaggerated or misleading for other sectors. We need to know, and the Commission needs to know in order to assess the degree of new unemployment which is likely to offset other job creation measures in the later 1990s.

We have only partial information on the new wave of foreign direct investment and the degree to which this will export jobs to central and eastern Europe, the United States and Asia. For the first time, this is concerning major German firms and a wide range of medium firms which hitherto have not gone multinational. For instance, the share of central and eastern Europe in the foreign direct investment of Italy has increased ten times from four to forty per cent of total FDI.

Much of this trend appears to be by medium-sized firms, which previously were locally based exporters from the home economy. Is this trend being replicated elsewhere in the Union? What are its effects on employment, granted that the SMEs constitute seventy per cent of enterprise employment?

The trend of more European firms adopting the Japanese just-in-time style links with suppliers on adjacent sites — such as the new FIAT Melfi plant — will have implications for the regional distribution of employment. We do not know what the effects will be in offsetting the effects of Objective I or Objective II of the Structural Funds.

Senior officials at Eurostat have stated that they lack the statistical base to answer many of the more relevant questions put to them by the Commission. We should be taking evidence from them, and asking what they need. DG V is engaging research into new methods of anticipating industrial change and its effects on employment and training. We should both support their intent and ask them what they are going to do.

Otherwise, while able to recommend a strategic framework for new employment, without better information we shall be joining the Commission and national governments in confronting new employment on side lights in the dark. Unless we can get more light on the situation we shall not know the political effects for ourselves, or for the Union, until they hit us.

Footnote

1. *Europe's Next Step: Organisational Innovation, Competition and Employment,* edited by Lars Erik Andreasen, Benjamin Corlat, Friso den Hertog and Raphael Kaplinsky, Frank Cass, 1995.

CHAPTER 10

Squaring the Circle

Stuart Holland

Aware that few if any institutions had quantified the unemployment effects of the financial convergence criteria for a single currency, we invited the Economic Council of the Labour Movement in Denmark and Alphametrics in Cambridge to make independent assessments, which it later proved were corroborated by a further report from the Observatoire Français des Conjonctures Économiques in Paris.

S.H.

*   *   *

Executive Summary

There is widespread disinterest and much disillusion with the European Union's two high profile strategies of the internal market and a single currency.

In practice these do not touch people in the preoccupations of their daily lives, especially security of employment for themselves and their families.

There also is strong feeling that joint Union policies are taking decision-making away from national governments and weakening democracy.

- *In fact the new power of foreign exchange markets and the multinational trend in trade and payments strengthens the case for a single currency.*
- *In turn this would strengthen democracy in the Union by restoring decision making to elected representatives rather than unelected speculators.*
- *Joint policies shaped through the new Surveillance Procedures can from now democratise strategic decision making by involving Union institutions, member states, regional and local government and the social partners in*

changed options for the economy and society.
But there needs to be a strategy which combines convergence
and cohesion. Such a strategy also needs to admit that the
deflationary effects of fulfilling the financial convergence
criteria for monetary union are draconian.

● *Every 10 per cent of debt reduction in the excess countries
  could reduce employment in the Union by up to one and
  a half million.*

● *Meeting the 60 per cent debt stock requirements in full
  could reduce employment by over ten millions.*

● *Meeting even the 3 per cent annual deficit targets by 1999
  would reduce employment by nearly a million.*

● *Fulfilling the 15 million jobs target of the Delors White
  Paper could need a gross job creation of some 20 millions.*

● *Closing the efficiency gap with leading competitors through
  transition to flexible production would create further
  unemployment in manufacturing.*

Squaring the circle of convergence and cohesion means a
perception and policy shift to realise that reducing unemployment is the key means to reducing national deficits and
debt. It also implies:

● *a major expansion of the European Investment Fund as a
  counter-cyclical instrument for cohesion;*

● *funding the expansion of the EIF by a share of the 6 per
  cent excess savings over investment in OECD Europe in
  recent years;*

● *rescheduling up to 300 billion of the 350 billion ecu
  currently spent by member states on unemployment and
  related benefits into employment creation.*

But new investment expenditures alone will not be enough.
A strategy for both convergence and cohesion implies:

● *reducing annual hours in at least bigger business and the
  public sphere to increase employment;*

● *negotiating such reduced hours in a manner which can
  reinforce choice of their working time for those at work and
  about to be employed;*

● *ensuring the social partners can offset inflationary
  pressures arising from higher employment.*

This is not a technical fix or trusting that in due course at
least some countries can realise the Maastricht financial

criteria. It implies both an active macroeconomic policy and mobilising policies for employment as a process of social negotiation of change itself.

In practice this means realising an implicit or explicit Social Contract for Cohesion:

- *between the Union and its citizens, through a commitment to ensure that the deflationary effects of Maastricht are offset by a high employment strategy;*
- *between the social partners at company level and in public administration.*

Its outcome depends not on the Union or member states alone but also on the social actors and citizens themselves. But this also could be its strength as individuals can see that their own actions, with others, in a democratised Europe, can affect their own future.

1. The case for monetary union

The case for a single currency in the Union is not only strong but stronger than is widely appreciated on several grounds.

– *The economic rationale*

The most standard case against monetary union is that nation states will need to resort to other instruments than exchange rate changes to adjust their trade balances, in particular higher interest rates and higher unemployment.

But a high share of trade now is multinational rather than international, by the same firms in different countries. Multinational companies have little incentive to follow through devaluation with lower prices on foreign markets where they are already producing and selling. To do so would be to compete against themselves.[1]

International trade now tends to be determined by foreign investment flows. Some four fifths of the US trade deficit is represented by autos and auto related components for Japanese plant in the US. Exchange rate changes alone will not remedy the structural surpluses and deficits which ensue. This lies behind the Japanese-US surplus-deficit.[2]

The new global competitive challenge cannot be met by devaluation alone even for those smaller and medium firms which still are local, regional or national rather than multinational. To compete long term Europe needs to close the efficiency gap with Japan and Asia, which means adaptation to new methods of work organisation and innovation.

Intra-Union devaluation brings short-term advantage to some firms in some countries, but at the cost of other countries. Italian exporters and component firms have done well from the recent lire devaluation against the DM. But more German firms are considering or undertaking investment outside the Union to offset the strong mark.

Such policies are damaging to cohesion and weaken the Union's employment base. Otherwise, as is well known, exchange rate uncertainty inhibits intra-Union trade, especially for small and medium firms. It raises both the risk and the foreign exchange cost of transactions.

In terms of some of the orders of magnitude cited later, it also is worth recollecting that the Commission's *One Market, One Money* report of 1990 estimated the potential savings in the foreign exchange reserves of member states from a single currency at some US$200 billions.

– The political rationale

The political rationale for monetary union and a single currency is both intra-Union and international.

For thirty years it has been evident that foreign exchange speculation can destabilise currencies, undermine the political mandate of elected governments, and wreck inter-governmental agreements. This occurred in the UK in 1966 and 1976. It occurred againt in France in 1983. It occurred again dramatically with the collapse of the exchange rate mechanism of the European monetary system in 1992.

Thirty years ago some 90 per cent of foreign exchange transactions were to finance trade rather than speculation against given rates. Now more than 90 per cent of such transactions are speculative.

Even the wider bands on the ERM since 1992 have not been able to offset the recent upwards pressure on the mark and downwards pressure on other currencies.

This is partly because of the increase in the sheer volume of speculative funds. When hundreds of billions of dollars are traded each day, central bank intervention to support given rates becomes increasingly unfeasible.

Arguably the Union should be prioritising international agreement for the incidence of a turnover tax on foreign exchange transactions. Even a very small rate could inhibit much speculative trade since so much of it operates on small margins. It may also be that such a turnover tax now is a precondition for stabilising exchange rates within the Union as a precondition for a single currency.

But the decisive answer within Europe to speculation against exchange rates is a single currency. In political terms, this would restore decisions on what is spent, why, how, when and by whom to elected representatives rather than unelected speculators.

Internationally, a single European currency should help stabilise world exchange rates. This would not of itself solve all of the new structural asymmetries in trade and payments. But it could be a keystone to the review of the functioning of the Bretton Woods institutions called for by President Clinton at the G7 Naples meeting.

In turn it could restore authority to those institutions to the degree that they related imbalanced trade to the recycling of global surpluses in the manner which was one of the main aims of the original Bretton Woods conference.

This offers potential for better balance not only between the Triad of the US, Europe and Japan but also better prospects for the reforming and developing economies.

2. The deficit and debt conditions

If the case for a single European currency is stronger on such grounds than widely appreciated, so is the potential deflationary impact of the deficit and debt conditions of the Maastricht Treaty.

To meet the Maastricht conditions, the member states must reduce their current budget deficits to 3 per cent of GDP and their gross debt to 60 per cent of GDP. But to cut current deficits at national level will restrain growth, income, tax revenue and job creation. To also reduce the excess on the stock of debt — without counterpart Union level expenditures — would throw the economies of the member states from recession into slump.

A 1993 study by the *Observatoire Français des Conjunctures Économiques* (OFCE) has made estimates on this for a Union of twelve for the period 1994 to 2000. The relevant figures are cited in Annex A.

It argues that, even if the target for monetary union were to be for only eight countries with the least debt excess to meet the 60 per cent debt target, this could involve taking nearly 5 per cent off Union GDP: from the rest of this year to end 1999 this would amount to one per cent of nominal GDP or 100 billion ecu per year. For the twelve member states before enlargement to do the same the depressive effect would be minus 1.95 per cent of GDP each year.

Combined with a deflation effect of 0.65 per cent to achieve annual deficit reductions, this would imply taking 2.6 per cent off GDP each year.[3]

In an analysis of the Italian case, cited in Annex B, Alphametrics (Cambridge) claims that public expenditure would need to be cut to 30 per cent of its 1994 level in real terms or — alternatively — tax rates would need to double. Their projections for both Belgium and Greece — two of the other countries wth the highest stock of debt — are very similar.

The effects on employment would be catastrophic.

The Danish Economic Council of the Labour Movement (ECLM) has just undertaken an analysis which indicates that reducing annual deficits to 3 per cent by 1999 would reduce employment by up to a million by 1998.

As illustrated in Table C.1 (in Annex C), their analysis of reducing the stock of debt by 2 per cent of nominal GDP in Belgium, the Netherlands, Italy and Sweden from this year to 1999 gives a reduction of employment of nearly one and a half million for these and other member states.[4]

As illustrated in Table C.2, the picture becomes dramatic if one extrapolates these assumptions to meeting the criterion of reducing the stock of debt to 60 per cent of GDP for Sweden, Finland, the Netherlands, Belgium, Italy and Spain.

Employment could be reduced on this account by over 10 millions.

In their own analysis, the authors of the OFCE study comment: 'Such a strategy seems to us suicidal'.

They then add that in their view: 'one must avoid giving the impression to financial markets that the countries which refuse to adopt (the strategy) give the impression to markets that they renounce monetary union . . . it seems to us vital to forget the budgetary criteria of the Treaty'.

But one cannot easily square the circle this way. If the convergence criteria just become an equivalent of the neglected Gramm Rudman budget deficit criteria in the US, one thereby questions not only the feasibility of monetary union but also the binding nature of other commitments in the Maastrict Treaty.

Nor would an increase in the Union's own resources solve the contradiction since they would come from national governments and would need to be financed either through higher taxation — which would be deflationary — or by further national borrowing, thereby further prejudicing the Maastricht criteria.

As the OFCE analysis admits, with major deflation prices and interest rates would fall. In this sense the inflation targets of the Maastricht criteria could be met. But this would imply massive social cost without even the full effect of the actual budget and borrowing cuts, since unemployment compensation costs would rise unless benefits also were cut.

Clearly there is scope for much more analysis and other views. There are limits to linear extrapolations, and different assumptions in different models. Discounting the heaviest debtors clearly would change the scale of the worst case scenario of Table C.2.

Nonetheless, what is striking is the coincidence between the orders of magnitude of these different findings. Even on annual deficit criteria alone, it is evident that countervailing action at Union level is needed to square the circle of convergence and cohesion.

3. The European Investment Fund and Union Bonds

It was to enable the Union to fulfil the convergence criteria without deflationary effects that the original proposal of the European Investment Fund was devised in 1992, thereafter being put to and endorsed by the Edinburgh European Council.[5]

– Offsetting national borrowing

The key point in this context is that the EIF's borrowing through Union Bonds does not count against national borrowing by member states, nor therefore on those states' public sector borrowing requirements, provided that the borrowings are not by governments themselves rather than by private or public companies, banks or other intermediaries.[6]

Also, the EIF is different from the Agricultural or Social or Structural Funds since it is a multilateral borrowing and lending institution, as if the IMF.

The Fund also was originally conceived as a macroeconomic instrument with extensive indirect effects, including promoting both economic recovery and economic and social cohesion.[7]

In this sense, it is misconceived to claim that when national governments are needing to hold back expenditure is not a time to increase it at Union level. If the Maastricht criteria are to be fulfilled it is vital that Union instruments such as the EIF should be expanded to compensate for the contraction of national budgets and borrowing.

There also are other gains from expanding Union financial instruments which do not count against national PSBRs.

To the degree to which companies in the new German Laender borrow from the Fund through Union Bonds to finance a major share of their reconstruction, this would reduce pressure on the federal budget and make possible a lowering of interest rates in both Germany and the rest of the Union.

Besides, the instruments do not need to be invented. Member governments agreed on them at Edinburgh. National parliaments already have amended the Rome Treaty in order to enable the Union to borrow and lend on its own account through the EIF.

The Fund's areas of expenditure include not only the transport and information trans European networks (TENs) but also energy, plus investment in urban regeneration (agreed at Copenhagen) and small and medium enterprise.

In an overwhelmingly urban society and an economy where some seventy per cent of employment is in SMEs, these areas are wide enough for the Fund to play a significant macroeconomic role in the European economy.

4. Offsetting the unemployment effects of the convergence criteria

In effect, if the Maastricht targets are to be met without ending the current recovery and throwing Europe into recession, then a major expansion of the Fund clearly is needed. But it has to be a macro financial instrument as opposed to the micro project finance of the European Investment Bank if it is to help achieve the dual targets of the financial convergence criteria of Maastricht and the major job creation vital to cohesion.

In October 1993 President Mitterrand called for a fund of 100 billion ecu to help counter unemployment. This call was then endorsed by Prime Minister Balladur.

In February this year it was confirmed to the European Parliament's Temporary Committee on Employment by the French Minister of Labour that this remained the official policy of the government, but that other member states were not agreed on the need for such a Fund of such a scale. They should be.

– Annual reduction offsets

As illustrated by the analysis of Annex D, a 100 becu Fund would be needed just to offset the deflationary effects of meeting the annual budget deficit target of 3 per cent a year between now and 1995. This could create the million jobs offsetting the near million job losses which otherwise would occur by fulfilling the annual deficit criterion.

– The EIF and cohesion

So far the expenditures of the EIF are not targeted on cohesion criteria. Nor should they all be, granted the scale of resources to be mobilised to offset deflation from fulfilling the financial convergence criteria of Maastricht.

On the other hand, there is a case for claiming that a share of the EIF's expenditures should be cohesion targeted in terms of unemployment rates and GDP levels to avoid aggravating interregional disparities within the Union.

Box E and Table E1 illustrate the case.

Germany would be the main beneficiary in absolute terms of a share of EIF lending based on cohesion criteria. Spain would be the second. The highest rates of increase in investment would be in Ireland, Portugal and Greece.

– *Stock of debt*

The orders of magnitude and the cohesion challenge increase if one considers the scale of Union expenditures which would be needed to offset the deflationary effects and possible 10 million job losses of meeting the 60 per cent debt stock criteria of Maastricht.

Not all the stock of debt need be transferred to Union financial instruments to avoid deflation. Italy is responsible for nearly half of the debt stock excess in the Union as a whole. Yet much of this reflects the fact that there is virtually no private pensions market in the country. People buy government bonds to finance their retirement. Arguably one of the really strong cases for privatisation in Europe now would be of this share of the Italian debt stock.

It nonetheless is clear that the debt stock reduction for other countries remains a key issue for Greece (Annex B) as well as for Belgium, the Netherlands and Sweden (Annex C).

Even an annual 2 per cent stock reduction from this year to 1999 in Belgium, the Netherlands, Italy and Sweden would increase unemployment in those countries and in the rest of Europe — through negative multipliers — by nearly one and a half million.

Offsetting even this target would need countervailing expenditures by the European Investment Fund of nearly 150 becu.

– *The 15 million jobs*

Besides, past experience indicates that to increase *net* employment requires much higher *gross* employment creation.

During the years 1985 to 1990 ten million jobs were created in the EU, but this reduced the unemployment rate by one quarter — from 10.8 per cent to 8.3 per cent.

Of the 10 million jobs created in the Union of Twelve between 1985 and 1990, 6.5 million went to women and 3.5 million to men. Women's participation rose from 43.5 per cent to 48.5 per cent.

This proportion was below that of the former EFTA countries and Japan. But it is open to question whether a similar increase in women's participation rates is possible in the current upswing, which would mean less job creation in this cycle than in the last.

The former 10 million increase was almost entirely in services. Employment in manufacturing rose by 1.5 million; in agriculture it fell by 1.8 million, while service employment rose by over 10 million.

Even assuming disregard for the convergence criteria of Maastricht, the above evidence indicates that to create 15 million jobs net may need 20 million new jobs gross.

To create enough employment to offset the deflationary conditions of the Maastricht convergence criteria and meet the Delors 15 million jobs target could need something in the order of 30 million jobs. Many of them will need to be in services.

5. Squaring the circle?

Does this mean one cannot square the circle of achieving a single currency and fulfilling the Delors 15 million jobs target?

Certainly not without countervailing policies on a major scale. Clearly not for all countries within five years. Possibly for all within seven years. Any of these schedules is ambitious.

A crucial point in this context is to realise that the convergence and employment objectives are not mutually exclusive but mutually dependent. Reducing unemployment is the best way to reduce budget deficits and debt. Nor does it depend wholly on new Union borrowing and expenditures.

What is needed are Union macro financial and economic policies to offset the effects of the convergence criteria combined with the cohesion objective of recovering a high level of employment by both investment expenditures and other means. The remit is in article 2, article 3a(1) and article 103.2 of Maastricht. The new Surveillance Procedures can democratise the debate on a rolling multi-annual basis.

Identifying the twin objectives within a new 2002 programme ten years on from the 1992 internal market agenda not only is worth consideration but may be vital to public support.

In turn this means gaining the confidence to realise that Europe counts in the sense that it can offer more to its members — both states and individuals — than they can achieve alone.

It also should mean a process in which governments can make plain that fulfilling the objectives of convergence and cohesion cannot be enacted simply at European Council level. Its success would involve both responsible action by the social partners and a host of local employment initiatives.

Can it be done without unanimous agreement of all member states?

In principle it could. Article 103.2 specifies that 'the Council shall, acting on a qualfied majority on a recommendation from the Commission, formulate a draft for the broad guidelines of the economic policies of the member states and of the Community . . .' ·

In practice, such use of a qualified majority could be divisive. One way of squaring the political circle could be for the IGC to consider a new 'enabling majority vote'. This would bind a qualified majority voting for it, and enable them to cooperate through Union institutions and with Union instruments relevant to the shared convergence and cohesion objectives. But it would not be binding on the minority.

If this appears bold, the contradictions of the present commitments to both convergence and cohesion should encourage boldness.

The alternative is dire. Drift without a clear strategy for both convergence and cohesion would too strongly echo the failure to respond decisively to events, which was typical of the interwar period. Racism and xenophobia spawn on unemployment. Low hope turns to no hope if people see no way in which the Union of Europe offers gains which reach themselves.

6. Internal demand, finance and high employment

For decades supporters of European Union have stressed the size of the internal market. The 1992 programme tried to make this real. But less attention has been paid to the degree to which the growth of this market depends on internal rather than export demand.

– *The importance of internal demand*

Stressing this in Annex D, the Economic Council of the Labour Movement also stress that the import share from countries outside Europe is less than 8 per cent of European GDP.

Exports have played a role in the recent recovery from negative growth in 1993, and there has been a positive and growing net export balance since that year.

This does not absolve underlying problems of competitiveness, addressed later. But the productivity gains possible from transition to more flexible production indicate that this can be redressed, albeit not without cost to some employment.

Essentially, the rate of growth of the European economy is largely for Europe itself to decide. A sustained rate of growth in turn would help sustain global economic growth, not least in the United States.

– *Savings into investment*

In macroeconomic terms, as also stressed in Annex F, there is an excess of savings over actual investment in OECD Europe equivalent to 6 per cent of its GDP. The highest share of this is in Italy, reflecting the pension provision from government bonds, indicated earlier.

This savings excess over investment amounts to some 400 billion ecu. If a share of such savings were translated into investment as part of a multi-annual programme for convergence and cohesion, it could help finance job creation.

Working from the benchmark employment assumptions of the ECLM analysis, if 400 billion ecu were deployed in investment this could in principle generate 4 million jobs. If raised through Union bonds and phased over the period to 2002 this would imply European Investment Fund expenditures of some 60 becu a year.

These figures are orders of magnitude. They need to be disaggregated for what investment with what probable effects. Account also needs to be taken of the range of jobs which would need to be created in services rather than in manufacturing, where some investment will displace rather than safeguard employment.

But they are feasible orders of magnitude in terms of the excess savings ratio obtaining now. There is money in these savings which should be translated into investment not least if it is to safeguard the value of the savings themselves.

– *International surpluses*
There also is a wider international implication of re-cycling trade surpluses into investment. This was one of the main aims of the original Bretton Woods conference. It is a key issue in terms of overcoming the structural nature of the US trade deficit with Japan.

For economic, political and also cultural reasons it is improbable that the US deficit with Japan can be remedied bi-laterally. But it could be triangulated via Europe whose import propensity from the US is higher than that of Japan.

To do this would mean realising the potential of the EIF and its Union bonds as an international borrowing instrument whose expenditures generate increased US-European trade and thereby take the pressure off the dollar, which cannot itself easily be remedied by exchange rate adjustment for the structural reasons illustrated at the outset.[8]

– *Creating jobs and reducing budget deficits*
One of the striking points which Michel Rocard has made to the Social Affairs Committee of the European Parliament is that the member states of the Union probably are spending as much as 350 billion ecu a year in unemployment benefit and other financial support schemes for the unemployed.

Allowing a margin for frictional unemployment compensation, this indicates a possible annual contribution of up to 300 becu from member states to create employment. In principle such a reallocation of expenditure could create 3 million jobs. In turn this would mean working people paying tax rather than claiming benefits.

Again, this is not to suggest that either the task is easy or the broad employment effect precise. But both the economic and political message should be clear. Shifting unemployment compensation into job creation both promotes cohesion and makes it easier to fulfil the financial convergence criteria for a single currency.

The balance of payments concerns of individual member states, if they were unilaterally to undertake such a programme, would be real. But, granted the low share of non-Union imports in total Union GDP, mutual exports should broadly offset mutual imports on a multi-lateral basis within the new convergence and cohesion strategy.

Estimates should be made of alternative scenarios on the trade effects for different groups of countries.

– Annual programmes and the multi-annual framework
It is important for the above argument to appreciate that the twin strategies of savings into investment and reducing unemployment compensation through job creation can and should be ongoing annual programmes.

As already stressed, estimating job creation from macro aggregates is not enough. If proposals and counter proposals were to be made by Union institutions within the framework of the new multi-annual surveillance procedures, the merits of different estimates and different arguments on the macro and micro sides could be both defined and refined.

What nonetheless is striking on the gross figures is that translating the equivalent of one year's 400 becu excess savings into investment, with the equivalent of translating 300 becu of unemployment compensation into new jobs could create 7 million jobs.

Annualised over seven years to 2002 would mean a target expenditure of 100 becu per year. It should not be inconceivable as a programme to 2002 that cumulative expenditures should double this to the annual equivalent of 200 becu.

On the gross figures this could generate something approaching the 15 million Delors jobs target, or half of the gross job creation of some 30 million plus jobs which would be needed both to achieve this and offset the full deflationary effects of the deficit and debt criteria for monetary convergence.

– *Investment, jobs and multipliers*
A further point is that not all these expenditures would need to be financed by Union bonds.

Union borrowing should be a means by which member states can use its resources as an *alternative and as a supplement* to their own expenditures.[9]

In turn this could register exceptional multiplier effects.

For instance, there are many investment projects in Europe which have gained technical, environmental or other planning permission but which have not been approved by Finance Ministries because they have outstripped their initial budget allocations.

If the EIF were to take over the national government contribution to such projects, and in cases where the national government was financing only half or a third or less of the project, the multipliers from EIF funding could be two, three or more.

There also would be indirect multipliers from a clear strategy for a major offsetting of the convergence targets by Union borrowing and expenditure. To the extent that supplier as well as contracting firms expanded orders, this in turn would stimulate private sector investment.

7. Inflation and unemployment
The Commission has tended to argue that once the Union grows for any period at rates above 2.5 per cent, inflation starts to reappear.

Clearly, this is a problem. But it is not clear that there now is a level for the old Paish-Philips trade-off or its later version as non-accelerating inflation rate of unemployment (NAIRU). In fact DG II, in their *Scenarios to 2000* document, have for the first time expressed misgivings about NAIRU as an operational guideline. They have good reason granted that we now face levels of unemployment of six, twelve or even twenty per cent in some member states before achieving non-accelerating inflation.

What appears to be happening is the emergence of structural and technological unemployment on a major scale, so that a much higher share of the labour force does not even enter into a cyclical employment-inflation trade-off.

The main point is that, to the degree to which the EIF or other Union instruments substituted for national borrowing, they would reduce national debt and interest rates. Nor should the Fund need to set higher rates than those in the stronger member states granted that its ecu denominated lending spreads risk over the ecu basket of currencies.

In this context it is interesting that in the technical annexes to their *Scenarios* document DG II argued:

'In order to compensate for the delay in economic recovery that an increased wage moderation would imply, the Edinburgh growth initiative is (i.e. is assumed to be) strengthened to an amount of ecu 30 billion in both 1994 and 1995 (60 billion cumulatively) in public works of Community interest and related fields'.

It added:

'Given the low rate of capacity utilisation in those years, no inflationary pressure should be expected of this package (which) would therefore fully support final demand without adverse effects, and would improve the logistic environment for private investment and thus would improve growth potential'.

Clearly this judgement can not simply be extrapolated in a linear manner. The higher the level of employment the greater the inflationary pressures are likely to be. But, as argued later in this paper, the issue is social rather than simply technical. It implies a challenge for the social partners whether they are prepared to trade-off sustained growth and higher employment for restrained wage and price increases. This can and should be posed within the rolling framework of the new Surveillance Procedures.

8. The wider challenge

The wider challenge concerns not only a working trade-off on wages and prices for sustained growth and employment. It also concerns the distribution of working time and productivity gains.

– *Redistributing working time*

Michel Rocard has forcefully argued the case for reducing the working week to the Social Affairs Committee of the Parliament.

Arguably reducing the working week would be inflexible. Probably, the Union should be thinking in terms of reducing annual hours with the right for working people to negotiate how such hours are reduced in a manner which reinforces not only their rights at work, but also their control over their non-working time.

For those with children or elderly relatives needing care, this may be so many weeks per year without overtime for that phase of their work life cycle. For others it could be fewer weeks earned from higher overtime. Reduced working time also could be related to further education and retraining, as is common in Denmark.

At macro level, there is econometric evidence from the Alphametrics team which argued that ten million jobs could be created in the Union of Twelve by reducing annual hours by up to 2.5 per cent within five years and up to 3.5 per cent over ten years.[10]

At individual level, the right within defined terms of reference to negotiate the personal incidence of such reduced hours could affect people's lives at work and in non-working time in a manner which increases real life choices in a manner never achieved by projects such as the 1992 internal market programme.

– *Harmonising annual hours*

The European Community has been committed since its inception to the principle of harmonisation. In the above sense there is no reason in principle why it should not seek harmonisation of maximal annual hours.

The case could not readily be introduced for all companies in all sectors. But its implications are significant for at least bigger business in the private sector and also for public administration and services. Nor could it in practice exclude second jobs for those in full time work at reduced annual hours, not least in the informal sector.

However, it could obtain for full-time jobs in companies over a given size as well as the public sector.

There also are indications that management is not averse to harmonising reduced annual hours. Some managers already have declared that they stand to gain in cases where workers in different subsidiaries work different hours provided that the policy also obtains for their competitors.

Indirectly, they also would gain inasmuch as harmonised hours would level the playing field for competition by efficiency, innovation and adaptation to new methods of work organisation rather than by lengthening working time for those already in work.

Like the cohesion implications of an expanded EIF, the policy also could appeal to broad sections of public opinion in Germany if the harmonised target for the Union aimed, after a transitional period, at 1500 hours per year [just below German average hours], and if this applied to all of the 12,000 plus firms in the Community employing more than 500 persons, including Japanese, US and other multinationals.

In this sense the harmonisation of reduced annual hours — involving individual negotiation, or options for different categories of workers — could fulfil the joint commitment of the Single European Act to both the internal market and cohesion.

The issues are wide ranging. The respective merits and demerits would need full evaluation and debate.

But granted (1) the limited scope for job creation through investment expenditures alone; (2) the degree to which the strategy would reinforce individual rights; (3) the imperative of ensuring that a higher share of the young enter the labour market, the Commission could be invited to formulate a draft directive for discussion both directly with the social partners and through the new Surveillance Procedures.

9. Closing the efficiency gap
and redistributing productivity

The question of what time for what pay then brings new dimensions to the question of inflation and trade-offs between the employed and wage levels.

It already is clear in notable cases such as Volkswagen that workers have preferred a four day week with less pay than a one in five chance of becoming unemployed.

But it is not at all clear that all reduced annual hours need to be accompanied by reduced pay.

The outcome will depend on the degree to which the Union is able to use policies such as the new Objective IV and ADAPT programmes to manage the transition to new methods of work organisation typical of leading Japanese firms and Japanese transplants in the US and Asia.

UK case studies of Lucas automotive components and of Rover Cowley show that output per worker has been *doubled* and *trebled* respectively by conscious adoption of such customised flexible production and economies of scope rather than old style and inflexible economies of standardised mass production. Similar gains appear to have been made at Peugeot.

The metaphor of one big leap and many small steps is constantly used by Rover management. Big leap to transition to flexible production. Many small steps through constant improvement *[kaizen]* thereafter.

Hyper-efficiency
The argument relates to the fact that not all of Japanese industry is hyper-efficient.

Ohmae has estimated that only 15 per cent of Japanese firms are hyper-efficient in the above sense. There also are major productivity disparities of 1 to 3 between even leading Japanese firms within the same sector.[11]

There are several implications for the competitiveness arguments of the Delors White Paper.

For instance, if 30 per cent of European manufacturing achieved a doubling of productivity within the typical range of transition to flexible production, this could restore aggregate productivity growth in the sector as a whole to 7 per cent per year, equivalent to its highest postwar 'miracle' growth rates.[12]

In turn, achieving such gains from flexible production implies a strategy for *strengthening* cooperation between management and labour rather than weakening the bargaining power of trade unions through flexible labour markets.

The bottom line for trades unions is that they cannot gain widespread agreement to reducing annual hours if this means corresponding cuts in pay. But such cuts are not needed in leading firms which can manage the transition to flexible production. There also is the macroeconomic case that cuts will reinforce recession.

In turn, when some companies can make productivity leaps of two to three hundred per cent, there are implications for redistribution of a share of the productivity gains through taxation to help extend the principle of shorter working time in other sectors where such gains are not readily feasible.

Such gains could in part be redistributed to more labour intensive services, not least social services, education and care for the young and the elderly.

Again, more analysis is needed of the relative effects. But the potential is considerable in a Union confident enough to launch such an agenda.

10. Democratising the debate

The institutions of the Union — backed by key national unions — should be able to get these issues on the agenda of the new Surveillance Procedures.

Potentially — by dynamising a rolling discussion on the annual economic and employment reports — the new procedures are a major advance which could democratise the whole debate on Europe's future granted that it gives the right to the European Parliament, the Committee of the Regions, the Economic and Social Committee and the Social Partners to input their arguments through the procedures for not only the Commission's budget but also for the the economies of the member states of the Union.

– Relevance to a new Social Contract

Bringing employment explicitly into the procedures — as now decided — should be not only a matter of comparing alternative scenarios but mobilising the case for what amounts to a European Social Contract.

Such a Social Contract should include both the right to work for citizens of the Union and the right to negotiate working time for those in bigger business and the public sector. But it also needs to address the issue of increased inflationary pressure with fuller employment.

This is not so much entirely new as reclaiming some of the best practice of the postwar past.

For much of the postwar period a Social Contract was implicit in the concern of governments to avoid a return to mass unemployment. It also had different forms in different countries.

To mobilise a Social Contract at European level from now, within the context of a joint strategy for convergence and cohesion, and through the new Surveillance Procedures, means interrelating several otherwise disparate arguments:

1. that full employment is feasible provided it is part of a project for the economy and society as a whole, in the context of strengthened policies for economic and social cohesion;
2. that reduced annual hours and increased rights to negotiate working time are an integral and major part of the project;
3. that transition to flexible production in the leading European firms will make possible productivity gains which can in part finance this programme and reinforce European competitiveness;
4. that monetary union not only offers gains to enterprise in offsetting exchange rate instability and transactions costs, but also strengthens the Union against foreign exchange speculation;
5. that this in turn can restore decision making on social expenditures and employment creation to elected representatives and governments;
6. that the expansion of borrowing and expenditures through the EIF and Union Bonds, combined with active employ-

ment policies by member states, can assist job creation while helping to fulfil the Maastricht convergence criteria for monetary union for most countries.

Footnotes

1. In an analysis of the second British postwar devaluation of 1967, Sir Douglas Hague and others found that less than a fifth of some 220 firms had lowered prices on foreign markets, and that most of them gave other reasons than devaluation for doing so. See further for this and more recent evidence in Stuart Holland, *The Global Economy*, Weidenfeld and Nicolson, 1987, chapter 5.
2. See further the United Nations Centre on Transnational Corporations, *The Triad in Foreign Investment*, New York, July 1991.
3. Observatoire Français des Conjonctures Economiques, *La Convergence en Europe: Bilan et Perspectives*, 93-02, Paris, October 1993.
4. Untitled paper by Henrik Hofman and Thomas Pedersen, Economic Council of the Labour Movement, Copenhagen, 20 April 1995.
5. Stuart Holland, *Economic and Social Cohesion in the 1990s*, Report to Commission President Delors and other Commissioners, 1992, published as *The European Imperative*, Spokesman Books, Nottingham, 1993.
6. This principle may be challenged in OECD. If so, it should be defended vigorously granted not only the magnitude of the issues involved but also the commitment to the objective of full employment in the Preamble to the World Trade Organization Treaty.
7. This was not only argued in the Cohesion report but also in the first Commission paper on the Fund (COM(93) 3 final 12 January 1993) which argued that: 'In the context of promoting economic recovery in Europe . . . the main objectives of the Fund will be to contribute to the strengthening of the internal market and the furthering of economic and social cohesion . . . by providing a complement or alternative recourse to government guarantees for infrastructure financing. The viability criterion will also be an essential element in its approach to SMEs.'
8. See further Stuart Holland, *Towards a New Bretton Woods: Alternatives for the Global Economy*, Spokesman Books, Nottingham, 1994.
9. This both was one of the main points made in the 1992 cohesion report and clearly was anticipated for infrastructural lending in the January 1993 Commission paper cit supra. The principle will need to be extended if future annual borrowing requirements are to be reduced significantly.
10. Stuart Holland, *The European Imperative*, op cit, pp 49-52.
11. Kenichi Ohmae, *Triad Power*, The Free Press, 1985.
12. See further, Stuart Holland, *Big Leap — Small Steps: the Implications of Post Fordism for European Productivity, Welfare and Employment*, Paper for the Cellule des Prospectives, October 1993.

Annex A

Table A1
Action needed to reach the 3 per cent public deficit level in 1999

	Reduction of Total GDP each year	Reduction of Public Expenditure as % of GDP
Germany	0,2	2,2
Denmark	0,4	1,7
Spain	1,6	2,6
France	0,6	5,6
Greece	0,9	2,7
Italy	1,0	3,5
United Kingdom	0,9	6,0
EU	-0,65	

Table A2
Action needed to realise the 60 per cent public debt level 1999

	Reduction of Total GDP each year	Reduction of Public Expenditure as % of GDP
Germany	0,6	2,2
Belgium	5,0	23,3
Denmark	1,4	7,9
Spain	2,0	4,4
France	1,4	7,1
Greece	3,0	13,2
Ireland	0,3	9,6
Italy	5,2	23,6
United Kingdom	0,9	5,9
EU	-1,95	

Source: OFCE.

Annex B

Meeting the Maastricht debt criterion— the Italian case, with implications for Belgium and Greece*

The attached table sets out alternative projections of GDP, public sector debt, taxation and the balance between them for Italy, which is one of three Member States where the problem of meeting the Maastricht conditions over the next 5-10 years is particularly acute, the others being Belgium and Greece. In all three of these countries, the most difficult problem to overcome concerns the scale of public sector debt which at present is substantially greater relative to GDP than the limit set in the

*Source: Alphametrics.

Maastricht Treaty (60% of GDP). To reduce this even close to the 60% figure within a comparatively brief period of time and without pushing up inflation seems impossible in respect of these countries.

Even on the highly implausible assumption that growth of GDP of 3% a year can be achieved over the next five years in Italy while the budget deficit is first reduced and then transformed into a surplus so that outstanding debt can be reduced without adding to money supply growth (ie without monetising the debt), the scale of the required cutback in public expenditure and/or increases in tax rates is enormous. If tax rates are held at their 1994 level (so that revenue is held down to 46% of GDP), expenditure would need to be reduced by over 40% in real terms to achieve sufficient budget surpluses to reduce debt sufficiently. Alternatively, the cutback could be divided between expenditure and taxes, but this would produce a no more plausible scenario, with, say, a 20% reduction in expenditure being combined with a rise of taxes of 10% of GDP.

Although the scale of what is required is substantial enough on this projection, once allowance is made for the inevitable repercussions of fiscal tightening on economic activity, the situation becomes even more problematic. Even assuming a relatively modest effect of any cut in public expenditure/increase in tax rates on GDP (fiscal tightening is assumed to reduce GDP relative to trend by 50% of the amount of the reduction in expenditure/increase in taxes involved), the attempt to achieve the Maastricht debt target by 1999 would result in a reduction in GDP of almost 10%.

At the same time, public expenditure would need to be cut back to only 30% of its 1994 level in real terms — or, alternatively, tax rates would need to double. The reason for this much greater degree of fiscal tightening is quite clear: as GDP is depressed by fiscal tightening, tax receipts are also depressed and the need to pay unemployment benefits is increased, so adding to the budget deficit and counteracting the attempt to reduce debt. As a consequence, either taxes have to be raised by even more or expenditure reduced even further to achieve the debt target, so further causing activity to decline.

The projections for both Belgium and Greece are very similar given that the scale of public sector debt is of the same order of magnitude in these countries as in Italy.

The conclusions for this exercise are clear. The scale of what is required in the form of fiscal tightening to achieve the Maastricht convergence condition for public sector debt for these three countries is wholly implausible. Any attempt to try to get close to the specified ceiling on debt would not only drive down the GDP in these countries but would be certain to have significantly depressing effects on the rest of the Community as markets for other countries' exports are diminished. The danger would be in setting off a cumulative process of decline in economic activity as each country tried to avoid increases in its own deficit caused by lower levels of economic activity by itself reducing public expenditure or raising taxes.

Table B1
Estimates of Maastricht convergence implications (ECU billion)

Italy with feedback and 3% growth pa						
	1994	*1995*	*1996*	*1997*	*1998*	*1999*
GDP	877	903	930	958	987	1017
Debt	1081	1081	1041	941	796	611
Tax	403	416	428	441	454	468
Expend	487	436	388	341	309	283
Balance	-83	-20	40	100	145	185
Italy with feedback						
GDP	877	847	823	809	801	801
Debt	1081	1081	1011	881	701	481
Tax	403	391	378	371	366	365
Expend	487	391	308	241	186	145
Balance	-87	0	70	130	180	220

Source: Alphametrics.

Annex C

1. Meeting the deficit and debt criteria of Maastricht*

At present only a few member states will be able to fulfil the Maastricht criteria by even 1999. Countries with public debt of more than 100 per cent of GDP will only be able to fulfil the debt criterion in the long term.

France has an immediate problem with the criterion of a public deficit on maximum 3 per cent of GDP. The deficit in

*Derived from the Economic Council of the Labour Movement, unpublished paper, Copenhagen, April 1995.

France on the general public budget in 1994 was 5.6 per cent of GDP. Countries like Sweden, Italy and Spain also have major problems with this deficit criterion.

A better growth outlook in Europe could help these countries to move closer to the target. But our calculations still show that in the short term this cyclical contribution will not be enough to achieve the Maastricht criteria. These countries will have to tighten their budgets dramatically if the debt criterion is to be reached in the medium term.

Public budgets will not be improved as much as the policy action predicates. This is because of built-in stabilisers (reductions in direct and indirect taxes and increases in unemployment expenditures) plus lower activity in the other European countries.

Table C.1 illustrates the employment effects of a simultaneous reduction in the public debt in Belgium, the Netherlands, Italy and Sweden.

The improvement in public debt is reached through a decrease in transfer incomes. The policy action results in a yearly 2 percentage points drop in the public debt ratio. So in the year 1999 public debt as per cent of GDP is 10 percentage points lower that the forecast value.

Table C1
Reduced employment effects of a 2 per cent annual reduction in the stock of debt

	1995	*1996*	*1997*	*1998*	*1999*
Belgium	-29	-59	-67	-76	-79
Netherlands	-54	-122	-162	-181	-186
Italy	-137	-193	-229	-244	-249
Sweden	-12	-35	-60	-82	-101
Rest of Europe	-419	-820	-967	-941	-844
Total of Europe	-651	-1229	-1485	-1524	-1459

Note: All the figures are in thousands and are deviations from the baseline.
Source: ECLM.

This policy action requires a greater decrease in the four countries budget deficit than the required decrease in public debt. This is because of the decreasing effect these policy actions have on GDP.

Employment drops by more than 0.6 millions in the four countries in 1999, with a further 0.8 million fall in the other European countries.

Reduced employment from meeting the Maastricht debt criterion

Table C.2 extrapolates the ECLM assumptions underlying the reduced employment caused by meeting the Maastricht 60 per cent of GDP stock of debt criterion for most of the major excess countries.

The countries are Sweden, Finland, the Netherlands, Belgium, Italy and Spain.

Unemployment falls from 1998 to 1999 due to assumptions of increased competitiveness from lowered wages with high unemployment.

Table C2
Reduced employment in Europe from the major excess countries fulfilling the 60 per cent debt reduction target

Reduced employment from fulfilling the Maastricht debt criterion

1995	-3,913,000
1996	-7,696,000
1997	-9,815,000
1998	-10,413,000
1999	-9,978,000

Source: Associate Research in Economy and Society, London.
Note: The figures are extrapolations from the ECLM model expressed as gross deviation in each year.

Annex D

A countervailing strategy*

One of the major problems with the convergence criteria in the Maastricht Treaty is the mechanical focus on the criteria. What is more important is the question of how to reach them in a sustainable way without risking further decreases in employment.

Some European countries have to improve their fiscal consolidation irrespective of the Maastricht treaty. This is the case for countries such as Italy and Sweden which have major

*Source: Economic Council of the Labour Movement, April 1995.

structural problems with their public budgets. But for most European countries, the deterioration of public budgets in 1992, 1993 and 1994 was caused by the downturn in economic activity in Europe.

A necessary condition for return to a higher growth path will be improvement in effective demand conditions in Europe. Higher levels of investment are needed, not least since public investment in recent years had been depressed in the wake of the recession.

Clearly, a higher investment effort at the national level can come into conflict with the Maastricht Treaty. One way to solve this problem is to implement a coordinated higher investment activity on a joint European basis through the Union bonds and the European Investment Fund as proposed in the December 1993 White Paper on *Growth, Competitiveness and Employment.*

Table D1 shows the effect of such a joint investment strategy, designed to offset the deflationary effects of reducing annual budget deficits to the 3 per cent Maastricht criterion.

The exercise shows that such coordinated investment could create a million jobs.

During the five years from 1995 to 1999, investment expenditures would total 100 becu. This is less than a third of what is needed before year 2000 according to the White Paper.

The yearly higher investment effort of 20 becu is in fact only 1/20 of the 6 per cent excess of savings over actual investment in the private sector.

Table D1
Stimulus from an expanded EIF. The effects for the European economy

	Decrease in public budget deficit (% of nominal GDP)	Increase in Employment (thousands)
1995	0.21	470
1996	0.32	850
1997	0.36	1070
1998	0.37	1110
1999	0.37	1050

Note:
1) Deviations from baseline
2) The Investment from the expanded EIF corresponds to 1/3 of one percentage of GDP in every year in each member state.
Source: Economic Council of the Labour Movement, Denmark.

Annex E

EIF lending, SMEs and cohesion*

To prove effective as a Union Public Sector Borrowing Requirement (PSBR) and expenditure instrument, it is vital that enterprises apply directly to the EIF rather than national governments. For larger firms this is straightforward. For smaller firms the Fund will need non-governmental national, regional and local intermediaries.

This is needed for borrowings not to count on national PSBRs. It also fits in the best sense with subsidiarity. It means relating the Fund directly to intermediaries at the regional and local level, including either banks or regional credit agencies and local enterprise or innovation centres.

The EIF already is in a position to offer incentived loans to SMEs. It also is foreseen that it will within two years be able to take equity holdings in such firms.

This is of the first importance granted the lack of a US style venture capital market in Europe. It also could improve on the US model inasmuch as there is evidence that venture capitalists frequently insist on bringing in larger firms for the expansion phase of a new product, with loss of control for the original entrepreneur.

But intermediaries in practice will be vital to the success of an expanded Fund. It needs to achieve some symbiosis with them if it is not to wait for applications which either do not occur from the SME sector, or which it cannot readily assess in terms of viability.

It also is important that the activities of an expanded Fund do not reinforce regional and other disparities in the Union. In this sense there is a case for considering that the Union should set indicative quantitative targets for at least a share of the Fund's lending which could be available on the basis of cohesion criteria.

Alternatively, such criteria for the Fund could be taken as benchmarks relative to the geographical incidence of other Union programmes as an indicator of convergence or divergence from its cohesion effects, and the need for other Union policies to offset these, such as Objective 1 and Objective 2 programmes.

*Source: Associate Research in Economy and Society and Alphametrics.

Certainly account should be taken of the degree to which different Union expenditures including the Fund do or do not promote cohesion. In this sense it is vital that expendtures do not replicate the kind of imbalance witnessed in the first ESPRIT programme, where over 70 per cent of the funds went to twelve major companies.

The following table illustrates an ECU 40 billion cohesion expenditure for a 100 becu annual EIF.

Table E1
Allocating a share of a 100 becu EIF on cohesion criteria

	Type of project SME TEN Other (billion ECU)			Total	Increase as per cent of existing rate of investment
	SME	TEN	Other	Total	
Denmark	0.2	0.1	0.1	0.4	2.5
France	2.3	1.7	1.3	5.4	2.6
Italy	2.8	1.1	1.3	5.2	2.7
Germany	4.4	3.4	1.8	9.6	3.2
Netherlands	0.8	0.6	0.4	1.7	3.2
UK	2.9	1.1	1.3	5.4	3.7
Belgium	0.5	0.5	0.2	1.3	3.8
Spain	3.3	2.5	0.9	6.6	5.4
Ireland	0.4	0.1	0.1	0.6	7.6
Portugal	1.2	0.4	0.2	1.8	7.8
Greece	1.3	0.5	0.2	2.0	12.4
Total	20.0	12.0	8.0	40.0	3.6

Note: SME share allocated on basis of cohesion criteria. TEN share takes account of geographical position in terms of Objective 1 and Objective 2 criteria. 'Other' allocated on basis of population.
Source: Alphametrics.

Annex F

Internal and export demand
in European economic growth*

Europe is now experiencing a recovery from one of the longest recessions in the postwar era. The growth rate in 1993 was negative. Output expanded again in 1994 and the outlook for 1995 shows a recovery well established. The recovery is boosted by an extraordinary help from growth outside Europe.

The main reason behind the recession is to be found in the development of final domestic demand in Europe. It is not

*Economic Council of the Labour Movement, Copenhagen, April 1995.

foreign trade which has worsened the employment situation. Net-exports gave in 1993 and 1994 a significant positive contribution to growth in GDP, cf. Table F1.

Table F1
Contributions to changes in real GDP growth in Europe. Per cent points

	1989	1992	1993	1994	1995
Final Domestic Demand	3,6	1,2	-0,6	1,2	2,4
Stockbuilding	-0,1	-0,1	-0,3	0,3	0,1
Net Exports	-0,1	0,0	0,9	0,8	0,5
Gross Domestic Product	3,4	1,1	-0,1	2,3	3,0

Note: Totals may not add up due to statistical discrepancy.
Source: OECD and Economic Council of the Labour Movement.

In 1989, the GDP rate was 3.4 per cent. Three years later in 1992 output growth was reduced to 1.1 percent and became negative in 1993. The main reason behind the lower growth rates was a fall in the contribution to output growth from final domestic demand from 3.6 per cent points in 1989 to -0.6 per cent points in 1993.

As shown in table F1, in 1993, the contribution from foreign trade was quite significant, at 0.9 per cent point, which helped to reduce the size of the downturn in 1993. Also in 1994 the positive contribution from trade has been quite significant.

The important point is that it was not foreign trade which caused the slow growth performance in the beginning of the 1990s. It was a totally 'home made' recession.

To understand the size of the downturn one should consider the development in employment. In the present downturn, employment in OECD Europe has been reduced by more than 7 millions which is *three* times more than what occurred during the downturn in the beginning of the 1980s.

Weakened economic activity has also had its cyclical counterpart in the position of public budgets. This is illustrated in figure F1 which shows the development in the position of the public budget in OECD Europe estimated in billion DM.

The data of Figure F1 demonstrates that there is a close connection between the growth rate and the government budget. In periods with declining growth the budget is aggravated whereas it is improved in periods with major growth rates.

Thus, a decisive way to improve public finance is through an increased growth in the economies of member states. Higher growth implies both lower transfer payments and higher tax revenues. When the recovery proceeds and matures in 1996, unemployment will fall, facilitating further reduction of national budget deficits.

To get a sustained growth and a major improvement in employment implies an expansion of domestic demand in Europe. Higher exports to the rest of the world have improved the outlook for the European economy. But to ensure sustained growth and higher employment means expanding domestic expenditure rather than relying on increased export demand.

Since over 70 per cent of trade in Europe is trade from one European country to another European country, the share of imports and exports excluding these intra-regional movements gives much smaller figures. Less than 30 per cent of OECD Europe's trade is trade from a country in the region to a country outside Europe. This means that the import-share from countries outside Europe is only 7-8 per cent of European GDP, which once again highlights the importance of the development in internal demand in Europe.

Figure F1
Economic Growth and Government Budgets. OECD-Europe

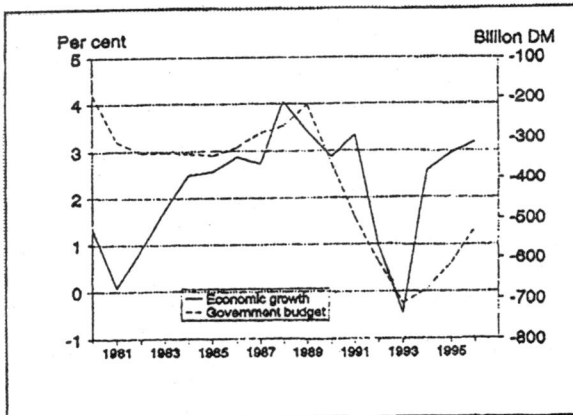

Source: OECD and Economic Council of the Labour Movement.

CHAPTER 11

Correspondence with Commissioner Bangemann

Commissioner Bangemann responded to the analysis contained in 'Squaring the Circle', which Mr Coates had sent to him.

Thank you for your letter of the 19th April 1995. I share your concern regarding social cohesion and the too high level of unemployment, and appreciate your efforts to focus on possible solutions in this field.

However, I doubt you are on the right track concerning the relation between convergence and employment. Being a complex issue and somewhat outside my area of responsibilities — although of general interest, and I would like to give you an answer — I took advice on this from the services of my colleague, Mr de Silguy, which explains why I forwarded him a copy of our correspondence.

In your letter you make reference to a recent Danish study and a somewhat older French one, both suggesting that the reduction of annual deficits according to the three per cent criteria should imply a contraction of GDP, and thus increase unemployment.

But you might as well refer to another Danish study, just published by the Danish Ministry of Economic Affairs ('Denmark in the Economic Cooperation in EU '95', March 1995, ISBN 87-601-4795-4, pages 79-82), or the IMF 'World Economic Outlook', October 1994, Annex II. Both present simulations showing that fiscal consolidation, eventually after an initial restrictive effect, increases medium term GDP growth.

The reason for this contradiction is the different models used. Pure Keynesian-demand type models produce the first set of results. Other models, like MULTIMOD, the IMF's international macroeconomic simulation model, allow for interest rates and exchange rates to change and influence investment and inflation, resulting in somewhat different and, in principle, more realistic results. This is also the case for the QUEST model used by the Commission services; see for example 'Scenarios to 2000' in *European Economy* No.55, 1993.

The position of the Commission concerning fiscal consolidation and employment is that at the current stage of the economic recovery there is no contradiction in macroeconomic policies to be recommended, as fiscal consolidation is called for to achieve sustained growth of GDP and employment, and to avoid repercussions due to adverse movements in exchange rates, interest rates, investment, inflation and a subsequent too tight monetary policy, enforced by this pessimistic scenario. I understand that President Santer has written to you along the same lines.

In short, the economic analysis you rely on in your letter is contradicted by other analysis and — I might add — the latter appears to be more in line with recent experiences. Ireland, for example, seems to be a good case in this respect, combining budget consolidation and high growth of GDP and employment.

Anyhow, I will be very interested in the results of the study you have commissioned by the NIESR, as well as I appreciate your promise to forward the two other reports you mention at the end of your letter.

*   *   *

Ken Coates replies to Commissioner Bangemann.

Mr Martin Bangemann   23rd June, 1995
Commission of the European Communities

Dear Mr Bangemann,

I really am very grateful to you for your letter of the 15th June, 1995. You have shown a keen appreciation of the problems which the Temporary Committee on Employment has been confronting, and I am especially pleased that you have drawn my attention to the Danish Finance Ministry study, of which I would not have been aware otherwise.

I am pleased that we share a common view on the need for social cohesion, and the reduction of unemployment levels.

As to the technical issues which are at stake, I, too, have asked for advice, both inside and outside the Temporary Committee which is seeking to understand these complex issues.

With one of the studies to which you refer us, we are already familiar. The paper, 'Scenarios to 2000' in *European Economy*, No.55 1993, was given to the Temporary Committee by DG II, and was already the subject of quite considerable discussion. You will find that it is extensively quoted in my paper 'Europe in Question', which has been circulated as an explanatory memorandum, with my draft Final Report for the Committee:

> 'In the technical annexes to their *Scenarios* document DG II argued: "In order to compensate for the delay in economic recovery that an increased wage moderation would imply, the Edinburgh growth initiative is (i.e. is assumed to be) strengthened to an amount of ecu 30 billion in both 1994 and 1995 (60 billion cumulatively) in public works of Community interest and related fields". It added: "Given the low rate of capacity utilisation in those years, no inflationary pressure should be expected of this package (which) would therefore fully support final demand without adverse effects, and would improve the logistic environment for private investment and thus would improve growth potential".'

In fact, this study is approximately the same age as the French one of the OFCE, which also appeared in October 1993. Because they had then presumed the need for compensatory action, DG II at that time encouraged a certain degree of optimism.

But when the proposed countervailing action is not taken, we fall back on far more dubious assumptions. The more recent DG II publication of January this year sustains its relatively optimistic forecasts on the basis of the hope that there will be a historically unprecedented increase in exports by member states. It does not appear to recognise any potential deflation of their mutual imports and exports as a result of the deficit and debt reduction to which they have committed themselves.

Further, the recent argument of the DG II analysis, that wage and price increases caused the recession of the early 1990s, does not fit the facts so well as do the correlations between developing recession and cuts in Government expenditure, which are charted by the ECLM in Annexe F of the Holland paper, *Squaring the Circle*.

I copied your letter to Dr Holland, and he has kindly sent me another paper which discusses the problems involved in these models. I think you will be interested in it, and I am enclosing it with this letter. It covers some of the same ground. In a nutshell, the MULTIMOD model is based on 'rational expectations perfect foresight' assumptions. These assumptions have been strongly questioned by Willem Buiter, an associate of James Tobin, the Nobel Prize winner. Buiter, cited in the accompanying paper, claims that this methodology is not empirically verifiable. I understand that such views have been widely accepted by economists, and that the model has thus been discredited. True, it still seems to be in use in the Danish Ministry of Finance and the IMF: but I am informed that the Bundesbank, which set up a similar model, has decided not to use it.

The IMF use of such models has not produced encouraging results. Where it has been applied through structural adjustment policies, through the 1980s, disastrous effects have been registered in low, middle income and highly indebted countries. Growth rates were almost halved, private consumption contracted five-fold, positive investment rates went negative, and imports contracted by up to three-quarters. None of this should have happened if the rational expectations and other assumptions of the MULTIMOD theory were correct. But even such drastic negative effects turned out to be insufficient to achieve the stated main objectives: to reduce debt and interest rates.

External debt as a share of GDP increased by two-thirds in the Middle East and North Africa, one-third in the already severely indebted countries, and by one-sixth in Latin America. Meanwhile, average interest rates actually increased for all the main countries concerned, despite public expenditure cuts. In practice, while rational expectations theory may not be empirically verifiable, it is clear that the assumptions implicit in these studies have been empirically falsified. The UNDP commented 'theoretically this should not have happened. The IMF and the World Bank were created in the 1940s specifically to avoid repeating the experience of the 1930s'.

I might be forgiven for suggesting that perhaps my earlier paper, 'Back to the 'Thirties?', is not so far wrong. It is corroborated by the Keynesian analysis of the OFCE in Paris, the ECLM in Denmark, and Alphametrics in Cambridge, and also by the negative example of the IMF track record, when it was most addicted to the pursuit of such policies during the 1980s. I feel sure that you will share my concern that the European Union cannot afford complacency about this issue. The notion that the reduction of debt and deficit will not register negative effects may read well in the Danish Finance Ministry and IMF models: but will it read well in practice, in the real economy?

My own conclusion is that it would be prudent to take action for an increase in Union bond borrowing and Union expenditures through the European Investment Fund, not least since there has been so rapid and positive a take-up of the initial 8 billion ecu package of the Edinburgh Facility by local authorities, energy and transport companies and others.

In this context I was impressed by the recommendation of an Edinburgh II package in that paper from DG II which you recommended to me in your letter, and to which I have already referred, which argues that a 60 billion ecu increase in the borrowing and expenditures of the Fund in 1994 and 1995 should have a zero inflationary effect and would fully support final demand without adverse effects.

Although we are more advanced in the current economic cycle than when that analysis was made, surely it remains relevant? Certainly the recommendation by the Commission of such an increase in the role of the Fund and Union bonds would be likely to signify recognition of concern and practical means of offsetting at least some of the deflationary effects of meeting the financial convergence conditions.

I also hope the Commission will consider the argument made by Stuart Holland in his paper *Squaring the Circle*, that if a share of such an expanded Fund were allocated on cohesion criteria, Germany would be the main beneficiary in absolute terms (a quarter) which would take pressure off the federal budget and make possible a lowering of interest rates for the Union as a whole. Meanwhile, the main beneficiaries in terms of increased rate of growth of investment would be the Objective 1 member states.

With my respect and good wishes.

Yours sincerely,

Ken Coates

*   *   *

There follow extracts from Stuart Holland's comments on the letter of Commissioner Bangemann on the employment impact of fulfilling the deficit and debt reduction criteria of the Treaty of Maastricht.

The Danish Finance Ministry and IMF models

Two documents recommended by Commissioner Bangemann are *Danmark I Det Okonomiske Samarbejde I EU '95*, of March this year and the IMF *World Economic Outlook* of October 1994. Both employ so-called-MULTIMOD models based on the theory of so-called 'rational expectations'.

It is surprising that DG II has such faith in these models. 'Rational expectations' theory became fashionable in the 1970s and early 1980s but has since been widely abandoned on grounds of highly restrictive and unrealistic assumptions.

The Danish Finance Ministry and the IMF are among a handful of institutions which still appear to rely on them. The Bundesbank, for instance, established such a model but then decided not to use it.

The analysis below demonstrates some of the main limits of such models from a scientific standpoint. The variance between them and Keynesian models in our context is not simply academic. It implies the risk of grave under-estimation of the employment effects of the Maastricht financial criteria and therefore is a major policy issue.

– *Rational Expectations*
The concept of rational expectations was introduced by Muth in 1961 and first applied to macroeconomics by Lucas in 1972, with further developments by Sargent and Wallace in the mid seventies.[1]

The *analytic* assumption of rational expectations is that at any given time firms' anticipations amount to 'true mathematical expectations' of the change implied by any course of government action at such a time. But this assumes that the private sector and the public sector all know each other's aims and anticipate each other's reactions *with perfect foresight.*

Against this pretension, they then assume that firms will discount public expenditure reductions by governments by assuming that such expenditure will in fact increase over the longer term.

– *Analogy with Voltaire's Candide*
In one of the more trenchant analyses of the limits of rational expectations models, Willem Buiter has compared the theory with the assumptions of Dr Pangloss in Voltaire's *Candide*.[2]

It assumes that all is for the best in the best of all possible market economies and that only wage or price surprises can cause the economy to diverge from a 'natural' rate of unemployment or a 'natural' level of output.

By contrast Buiter — who has done much of his criticism of rational expectations models with Nobel Prize Winner James Tobin — concludes that:

> *'There is no reasonable case that . . . monetary and fiscal policy rules cannot alter the cyclical fluctuations of the economic system or the nature of its trend growing path.*
>
> *'There is no presumption at all that a government that sits on its hands . . . is guaranteed to bring about the best of all possible worlds'.*

– Unscientific basis

Buiter adds that the rational expectations hypothesis is seldom tested in isolation rather than in combination with a range of other hypotheses, and that it is:

> *'in danger of being consistent with any conceivable body of empirical evidence, because the assumption of optimal use of the available information cannot be tested independently of an assumption about the available information set'.*

He adds because the hypothesis is not amenable to empirical verification it:

> *'cease(s) to belong to the realm of scientific (positive or empirical) theory as defined by Popper'.*

The deflationary effects of IMF and World Bank policies

In July 1994 the G7 Summit at Naples endorsed President Clinton's call to undertake a multilateral review of the functioning of the IMF and the World Bank. The background to the plan to review the IMF and World Bank was reported to be disappointment of the administration with their performance in reforming the Russian economy and their failure to help Africa and Latin America.

The President had good reason for such claims. The effects of structural adjustment policies in such regions of the world economy have been highly negative for investment, employment and trade in a manner which the Union cannot afford to replicate through unconstrained fulfilment of the budget and borrowing conditions of the financial convergence criteria of Maastricht.

– The failure of structural adjustment

Since the 1970s there have been three main dimensions to the IMF/World Bank strategy for structural adjustment. They amount to a varying combination of devaluation, deflation and deregulation justified in substantial part by rational expectations theory.

The formula is not entirely denied within the Fund or the Bank themselves. Rather they maintain that they need a standard adjustment package for countries which implies impartiality and lack of prejudice.

But in practice the package is prejudiced in the sense that it prejudges the mechanisms by which adjustment should take place, as does rational expectations theory.

Such reasoning was heightened with changed appointments at senior levels in the economic staff of the Fund in the 1980s and the increased emphasis given to rational expectations theory and assumptions of market clearing with appropriate prices and exchange rates.

It was reinforced by the fact that whereas the developing countries gained recycled OPEC surpluses in the later seventies, the second oil shock of 1979 compounded slower economic growth in the developed countries with a raised real cost of debt service.

The result has tended to be a beggar-my-neighbour syndrome of deflation and debt, compounded by competitive devaluations. Deregulation has not raised international competitiveness, and in many cases has been used in the form of debt-equity swaps in a manner which has reduced a fraction of the debt burden of less developed countries by selling their better performing assets to foreign banks and firms.

– *The disaster decade*

This became most evident in the disastrous decade in which monetarist reasoning and rational expectations theory became dominant in the Fund, and to a lesser but significant degree, in the Bank.

The World Bank's *World Development Report* for 1992 shows that the average annual growth rate of the low and middle income countries almost *halved* in the 1980s relative to the previous fifteen years, while growth rates of over 6 per cent collapsed for the Middle East, Africa, Latin America and the Caribbean, as well as the severely indebted countries.

The World Bank report shows *a five-fold compression* in the 1980s in the annual rate of growth of private consumption in Sub-Saharan Africa, Latin America and the Caribbean, and the severely indebted countries.

It also shows that high positive annual rates of growth of gross domestic investment from 1965 to 1980 were translated into draconian *disinvestment* in the same regional groups and categories in the 1980s, with an annual contraction of 13 per cent in Sub-Saharan Africa and 12 per cent in Latin America and the Caribbean, and the severely indebted countries.

Likewise, the force of *import contraction* in the same regions and categories went strongly negative in the 1980s, with annual average falls of three-quarters for the lower and middle income countries as a whole.

Meanwhile, even such cutback production, compressed demand, disinvestment and import contraction were *not sufficient to remedy external debt* as a share of GNP. Between 1980 and 1990 this more than tripled in Sub-Saharan Africa, increased by two-thirds in the Middle East and North Africa, by a sixth in Latin America and the Caribbean and by a third in the severely indebted countries.

Moreover, *average interest rates increased* for all of the main regions and the severely indebted countries, while public loans with variable interest rates soared as a share of total public debt.

– Deflation and negative transfers

Some officials in the Fund and the Bank disclaim their own responsibility for such a disastrous record in the low and middle income regions of the world economy.

Their main defence is to claim that the 1980s was the decade in which such countries needed to face the consequences of the debt which they had engaged as private banks recycled the OPEC surpluses which followed the first oil shock in 1973. Another is to claim that the countries concerned had misused such borrowing and failed to achieve soundly based growth.

In fact it was the deflationary monetary policies adopted by the G7 other than Japan following the second oil shock which (i) slowed global economic growth; (ii) raised real interest rates; (iii) precipitated the Latin American debt crisis of 1982, which in turn meant (iv) the collapse of private lending to the developing countries.

The collapse was seismic. But it was reinforced rather than countered by a parallel collapse in the IMF's lending. Between

1983 and 1987, net IMF transfers to developing countries turned from plus $7.6 billion to minus $7.9 billion.

Further, World Bank transfers moved in much the same direction (despite the softening influence of concessional lending through the IDA). In 1991, net World Bank transfers were minus $1.7 billion.

As the UNDP Development Report for 1992[3] comments:

> Theoretically, this should not have happened. The IMF and the World Bank were created in the 1940s specifically to avoid repeating the experience of the 1930s. They were supposed to intervene in order to moderate the extreme cycles of unregulated financial markets . . . Far from dampening the cycles, they amplified them.[4]

The record of these policies in these countries is a demonstration of Buiter's claims that rationale expectations theory is unscientific.

I submit that the European Union cannot afford to be complacent in the face of such evidence of negative effects on those real economies where policy makers assumed — in line with rational expectations theory — that reducing budget deficits and debt would have no effects on the real economy or employment.

Footnotes

1. Muth, J.F., Rational Expectations and the Theory of Price Movements, *Econometrica*, Vol.29, July 1961; Lucas, R.E., Econometric Testing of the Natural Rate Hypothesis, *Journal of Economic Theory* Vol.4, April 1972; Sargent T.J. and Wallace N, Rational expectations, the Optimal Monetary Instrument and the Optimal Money Supply Rule, *Journal of Political Economy*, Vol.83, April 1975 and Rational Expectations and the Theory of Economic Policy, *Journal of Monetary Economics*, Vol.84, April 1976.
2. Willem Buiter, *The Macroeconomics of Dr Pangloss: a Critical Survey of the New Classical Macroeconomics*, The Economic Journal, Vol.90, March 1980.
3. United Nations Development Programme (UNDP), *Human Development Report 1992*, New York/Oxford, Oxford University Press, 1992.
4. *Ibid.*, p.51.

CHAPTER 12

President Santer's Response

The President of the European Commission wrote in the following terms to Mr Coates about 'Squaring the Circle'.

As I promised in my letter to you of 31 May, the Commission's Directorate General for 'Economic and Financial Affairs' has now examined Mr Holland's report. As a result, I am pleased to note that the measures proposed in the report are largely in line with the Commission's approach to the unemployment problem.

However, the relevant services do have some reservations concerning the paper's analysis of the link between public finance adjustments and employment behaviour.

A sound and stable macroeconomic environment is a precondition for long-term growth and the creation of employment. Given the high debt and deficit levels presently observed in a number of member states, budgetary consolidation would still be necessary even in the absence of the convergence criteria laid down in the Maastricht Treaty. High budget deficits may result in public debt unsustainability, which would undermine growth and lead to difficulties in conducting stabilisation policies. By looking exclusively at the demand side of the economy, the paper seems to neglect the fact that the reduction of public debt and deficits has a favourable effect on the overall economic environment and helps to re-establish a positive business climate. Indeed, as stressed in the White Paper, the fall in interest rates to be expected as a consequence of budgetary consolidation — an effect that is also predicted in the OFCE study quoted in Mr Holland's report — is likely to stimulate investment. The increase in business confidence will strengthen the positive effects on investment.

Experience shows that a credible budgetary consolidation strategy can go hand in hand with *higher, not lower economic growth and employment.* The best example is Ireland which has managed to dramatically reduce its government deficit from 8.5 per cent of GDP in 1987 to 2.2 per cent of GDP in 1990, and has brought down public debt at an impressive speed. In spite of the deficit reduction, the recession still present in 1986 turned into a boom. Between 1987 and 1990 GDP grew at an average annual rate of 6.5 per cent. In 1994 and 1995 the government deficit has remained well below 3 per cent of GDP and is forecast to do so in 1996.

Meanwhile, total employment has grown at a rate of 2.6 per cent, with a similar trend likely in the future, thus showing a much better performance than the EU average. In last year's Excessive Deficit Procedure, Ireland was one of the two countries not found to have an excessive government deficit.

Another example of a successful consolidation strategy in the 1980s is that of Denmark. In both cases, crowding-in effects and the positive impact on economic agents' confidence dominated over the potentially negative effects of a reduction in government expenditure.

Member states should take advantage of the present phase of the business cycle in order to reduce budgetary imbalances. Given the current expansion of economic activity, employing the EIF to boost demand, as proposed in the report, would clearly be ill-timed. Moreover, the EIF, like the other investment support mechanisms mentioned in my letter of 7 April, was neither designed nor should be considered as a counter-cyclical instrument.

In spite of the above considerations, I fully share your concern that EMU should not have any negative effects on employment and can assure you of the high priority that solving Europe's problems of high unemployment has on the Commission's agenda. Indeed, the White Paper on Growth, Competitiveness and Employment, as well as the conclusions from the Essen European Council reflect the importance of this issue. The October report by the Commission to the European Council will also tackle most of the problems addressed in Mr Holland's study. In particular, active labour market policies will be identified as a key element of the strategy to increase employment.

Moreover, the Commission's Cohesion Report, to be published towards the end of this year, will raise the issue of how to reduce the disparities between levels of development in the various regions of the Union. The strategy of combining convergence and cohesion proposed in Mr Holland's paper is, therefore, broadly in line with the Commission's approach.

Lastly, I fully agree with Mr Holland's concern about the potential inflationary pressures of higher employment. The role of the social partners is of paramount importance for finding appropriate and socially acceptable solutions to this. The Commission has taken account of their crucial role by embodying 'The Social Partners' guidelines for turning the recovery into a sustained and job-creating growth process' into its 1995 Broad Guidelines.

*   *   *

Mr Coates replied to President Santer as follows.

Mr Jacques Santer,   3rd July, 1995
President,
European Commission

Dear Mr President,

I am very grateful for your further letter of the 22nd June, and for its assurance that the Commission remains committed to 'the strategy of combining convergence and cohesion'.

We are both aware that there is some difficulty in the combined pursuit of these different objectives. For this reason I took your remarks about the examples of Denmark and Ireland very seriously. My attention had previously been drawn, by Mr Bangemann, to a study by the Danish Finance Ministry. When I began to look at this case in detail, it seemed to me that neither the Danish nor the Irish cases could be deemed an unqualified success. True, there was some improvement in terms of growth: but this was combined with major increases in unemployment. Let me examine the two cases in more detail.

1. Denmark

In Denmark the deflationary measures undertaken by the government from the mid-1980s caused:

- a recession from 1986/87 to 1993 which was the longest not only in the postwar history of the country but of any industrialised country since the war;
- an increase in unemployment of *nearly sixty per cent* from 220,000 in 1987 to 350,000 in 1993.

It is difficult to reconcile these draconian results with the zero impact on employment expected from the Danish Finance Ministry model and its rational expectations assumptions on which our own DG II appear to be relying.

Rather, the sixty per cent actual increase *coincides almost exactly* with the kind of increase in unemployment which comes from the Holland extrapolation from the ECLM model for the Union as a whole.

Does it not appear likely that the negative result in the first Danish referendum may not have been unrelated to the very substantial increase in unemployment over the previous years?

Against the assumption that 'all will be for the best' encouraged in the forecasts of the Danish Finance Ministry model, the actual Danish experience points to the contrary judgement. The European project may itself be questioned by even more of its citizens — not least in referendums — if attempts are made to meet the budget and borrowing conditions of Maastricht without any countervailing policies embodying the concern of the Commission and the Union to defend and extend employment. These we have frequently itemised: expanding the borrowing instruments such as the EIF — as called for by President Chirac — and addressing the reduction of annual hours, which itself could create ten million jobs.

In addition, one of the main reasons why the contraction of the Danish economy was relatively restrained (in contrast to what might have happened) was the continuation of very high levels of unemployment benefit — up to eighty per cent of previous income for up to seven years. Had this not been the case, demand and growth would have been lower. Yet such high social protection does not exist in most member states.

2. Ireland

In Ireland, there was impressive GDP growth between 1987 and 1990. But unemployment increased from just under a quarter of a million in 1987 to just under 300,000 in 1993. *Long term unemployment doubled* during this period, to nearly 200,000.

This in itself corroborates one of the main claims made by the Temporary Committee, that the link between investment, growth and employment has been broken.

I submit that this evidence should cause us grave concern, for it has implications for the Union as a whole, as you yourself imply. The Union economies are unlikely to grow — even without deflationary effects from meeting the financial convergence criteria — at much more than three per cent a year, even making heroic assumptions about growth in the US and competitiveness in relation to Asia.

Yet while its growth rates peaked at more than *double* this rate, unemployment in Ireland increased by twenty per cent. This, in an economy where the total level of registered unemployment already approached one person in five.

In your letter you cite Ireland as the best example of evidence from experience that a credible budgetary consolidation strategy can go hand in hand with higher, not lower economic growth and employment. But if we extrapolate this best example as a model for the rest of the Union at a more realistic three per cent growth rate, this would imply an increase in unemployment for the Union as a whole, of between *seven and eight millions.*

3. Country cases versus Union effects of fulfilling the criteria

A further reason why I think we should reconsider both what happened in Ireland and Denmark is that their fiscal adjustments were undertaken during the 1980s at a time when the economies of the other member states of the Union were growing strongly.

Their growth would not have been possible if even a significant number of leading member states were cutting deficits and debt at the same time.

Buiter, Corsetti and Roubini stress this in a survey of case studies of estimating the effects of financial convergence, calling it 'the concurrent effect', meaning simultaneous contraction rather than competitiveness.[1]

As they claim: 'An announced sequence of fiscal tightening could initially be expansionary only if its expected severity escalated over time; in practice this is unlikely to be sufficient to reverse the concurrent effect, even at the beginning. We conclude that transition to EMU is likely to be deflationary in the EC. Three independent model simulations by the OECD (Englander and Egebo, 1992) using INTERLINK, by Giovannini and McKibbin (1992) using the MSG model, and by the IMF (in a confidential study) support this conclusion'.[2]

Buiter and his colleagues stress that the orders of magnitude in the different simulations vary considerably. But in our context it is impressive (or depressing) that *all of these estimations — including that of the IMF — indicate negative effects.*

What this means is that the more countries seek to fulfil the conditions, the less relevant are the Danish and Irish examples in terms of GDP growth, while the already high increases in unemployment during their stabilisation programmes in the late eighties and early nineties would have been still higher yet, in a general context of fiscal severity.

4. Changes in exchange rates

A further factor in both the Danish and Irish cases was devaluation. In the Danish case, this was by twenty per cent before stabilisation and in the Irish case in line with the devaluation of sterling on Black Wednesday.

Such devaluations were highly significant for the export growth rates of both countries and also for GDP growth.

But devaluation would be ruled out in the approach to a single currency. In which case, again, the general relevance of the Danish and Irish cases in terms of GDP growth is itself devalued as a model for the rest of the Union.

5. Interest rates and costs

The several studies cited in the Holland paper did not only look at the demand side of the economy. For instance, the ECLM model assumes increased competitiveness from lower wage costs with higher unemployment and also allows for the impact of lower interest rates. The OFCE study does admit lower interest rates, as you say in your letter, but also forecasts a collapse of growth which it calls 'suicidal'.

6. The heavily indebted member states

So far I have had no response which I can transmit to the Temporary Employment Committee from DG II on the Alphametrics analysis of the Italian case, that Italy's fulfilment of the criteria is out of the question.

In this context DG II also might care to respond to Giovannini's and McKibbin's assessments that Italy 'gets slaughtered' on impact, with an output fall of eleven per cent of GDP.

DG II also may wish to comment on the assessment of Buiter and his colleagues that if the seven most heavily indebted member states were to move only halfway to the sixty per cent debt target this would involve 'dangerous fiscal overkill'.

7. Unprecedented export growth

Similarly, as yet I have had no answer which I can refer to the Committee on how DG II expects a historically un-precedented increase in exports by member states — seventy per cent of whose trade is with themselves — at a time when most of them would be cutting back on domestic demand and thus mutual imports if they were seeking to fulfil the financial criteria for a single currency.

8. Theory and practice

I agree with you that the results one gets from models depend very much on their assumptions — whether Keynesian, monetarist, rational in their expectations or otherwise.

But surely we must ponder the fact that the two country studies which you have drawn to my attention as best case examples have in fact resulted in major increases in unemployment under conditions where their exports and growth were favoured through devaluation and sustained growth elsewhere in the Union. These are growth conditions which would not obtain if all or even most member states were to adopt deflationary policies at the same time, and where devaluation would be ruled out in the period of transition to a single currency.

Surely we cannot avoid the recognition that *the evidence of what actually happened to unemployment in both Denmark and Ireland clearly fits the Keynesian rather than monetarist/rational expectations case — and econometric models?* And this concerns events and conditions more favourable than those which would obtain in the prelude to implementation of a single currency.

9. Implications

The Danish and Irish cases do not in fact reassure. They give rise to serious misgivings.

I think perhaps we are being given one-sided advice and examples, which need to be tested against the kind of criticism implied in the alternative studies, which we have been considering in this discussion. But much more seriously, if the weight of partial advice led us to take no countervailing action, this could undermine the viability of monetary union, and the Maastricht objectives of a high level of employment and rising living standards. With such losses, might we not also lose the credibility of the European project to our electorates?

Is it beyond the bounds of possibility for you and other Commissioners, in this context, to give the most serious consideration to the submission of President Chirac, following the call of President Mitterrand, for an expansion of the borrowing and expenditures of the European Investment Fund and for consideration of one of the main means of gaining a significant increase in employment in the Union — reducing working time in at least bigger business and the social sector.

10. The Commission and the Council

Such a response to President Chirac on the Fund would surely give a signal from the Commission that it recognises the need to expand Union financial instruments in a manner which would not only thaw the freeze on the TENs, but also fulfil the Council agreement at Edinburgh and Copenahgen that *the Fund should contribute finance for the TENs, for energy projects, for venture capital loans and equity finance for SMEs, and also for urban renewal.*

Not least, an expansion of the resources of the Fund would be vital to ensure that the Cannes agreement on Local Employment Initiatives can be funded on a scale which meets their ambitious targets. The urban renewal remit for the Fund agreed at Copenhagen could cover many or most of these.

The six per cent excess savings over actual investment in OECD Europe should be tapped, much on the lines of the recommendation of the earlier Scenarios 2000 document from DG II which recommended a sixty billion ecu increase over two years in the Fund's borrowings and expenditures.

The fear otherwise is that the Local Employment Initiatives will run the same risk as the TENs of expectations not being realised because of budget limits.

I appreciate that at present there is limited support for an expansion of the Fund in the Council. But I submit that this has been highly influenced by both the recent stance and current problems of the British government. Several other heads of government are known to appreciate the merits of the case.

Serious consideration should be given to the proposal by Dr Holland in his 'Squaring the Circle' paper of *a new enabling majority vote* which would mean that those member states gaining a qualified majority for a new policy should be able to call on Union institutions to support and help fulfil it, without the minority being bound by the decision.

In the case of the European Investment Fund this would mean that an increase in its borrowings and expenditures would be available for projects within those member states which voted for it, without binding those member governments which voted against such an expansion or allowing them to draw on the increased resources which became available.

If we are to erode Euro-scepticism and challenge Europhobia, we certainly need to show that the Commission is concerned about the risk of potential employment loss from monetary union and is prepared to make recommendations to the Council which will be meaningful for millions of people who at present see no way in which deepening integration will defend their jobs or extend their rights.

That is why I would be strongly reassured if the Commission were able to formulate and publicise a recommendation to the Madrid Council for a significant expansion of the role of the Fund as well as a draft directive discussion by member states and the social partners on the reduction of working time.

I think you may share my assessment that this could persuade a significant body of opinion within the European Parliament and its committees that their concerns, on behalf of those who elected them, now are being recognised.

With my respect and good wishes.

Yours sincerely,

Ken Coates

Footnotes

1. Willem Buiter, Giancarlo Corsetti and Nouriel Roubini, 'Excessive Deficits: Sense and Nonsense in the Treaty of Maastricht', in *Economic Policy*, April 1993, Cambridge University Press and Editions de la Maison des Sciences de l'Homme, pp. 58-99.
2. Englander E.S. and Egebo T, 'Adjustment Under Fixed Exchange Rates: Application to the European Monetary Union', OECD Economics Department Working Papers, No.117, 1992; Giovannini A. and McKibbin W, 'The Economic Consequences of Maastricht', Mimeo, May 1992.

CHAPTER 13

Democratising the Debate

On the 8th March 1995, the European Commission published a communication to the Council of Ministers under the title 'Follow-up to the Essen European Council on Employment (Com (95) 74 Final)'. This proposed a framework for surveillance procedures by which the European Parliament, the Social Partners, and the Committee of the Regions and Local Government can monitor progress in job creation, and in reducing unemployment. The Council endorsed the proposal. For the first time, these procedures also offer a rolling framework to democratise the debate on both employment and the economic policies of the member states, as well as the Commission. This had been called for in the first report from the Temporary Employment Committee, before Essen.

K.C. & S.H.

Introduction

1. Fighting unemployment is a paramount task of the European Community and its Member States (arts. 2, 102a and 118 of the Treaty). In December 1993, the Commission's White Paper on *Growth, Competitiveness and Employment* proposed a series of policy actions designed to increase competitiveness, strengthen economic growth and turn that growth into more jobs through structural changes in Member States. As the White Paper has underlined, it is possible to significantly reduce unemployment but continued efforts will be necessary for many years. Progress in reducing unemployment levels is essential if the construction of Europe and the transition to Economic and Monetary Union are to continue to receive the support of European citizens.

2. The conclusions of the European Council (Dec. '93) endorsed this approach and identified key areas of action. The conclusions of the European Council at Corfu and then at Essen (Dec. 94) gave a further dynamic to the ideas set out in the White Paper and consolidated the Employment Action Plan by setting out five key areas of action. The Essen conclusions also broke new ground in the employment field, urging the Member States to *'transpose these recommendations in their individual policies into a multi-annual programme having regard to the specific features of their economic and social situation'.*

3. In order to pursue these objectives, the Essen European Council requested *'the Labour and Social Affairs and Economic and Financial Affairs Councils and the Commission to keep close track of employment trends, monitor the relevant policies of the Member States and report annually to the European Council on further progress on the employment market, starting in December 1995'.*

4. These objectives and principles therefore now need to be translated into practice, in terms of both action by each Member State, and in terms of further developing co-operative policy-making. This communication proposes orientations regarding these different points with a view to progressively instituting a process of surveillance of the functioning of the employment system as defined in the White Paper *'Growth, Competitiveness, Employment'.*

A coherent approach

5. The Commission considers that the next phase of co-operation between the Member States and the Commission should involve a coherent approach by the Economic and Financial Affairs Council and the Social Affairs Council, culminating in the European Council, thus avoiding a 'two track' approach to policies and based on an interdependent set of macro-economic and structural policy initiatives. This approach is essential because most issues which affect employment are inter-related and concern different policy responsibilities, e.g. non-wage

costs involve issues of competitiveness, public finance, as well as social protection, just as human resource development involves various policy and financial concerns.

6. To achieve this goal, it would be useful to:
   - develop this coherent approach on employment in the context of Article 103 of the Treaty.
   - identify the key characteristics of employment performance, with particular reference to the five action points of the Essen conclusions, that could be used by all concerned both in establishing the individual Member State multi-annual programmes and in monitoring the progress of Member States and the Community as a whole.
   - identify with Member States the essential elements and factors for the adaptation of education and training systems and support actions for their development, including 'good practices' in the area.
   - include in the medium-term programmes of Member States and/or in their convergence programmes, where this is not yet the case, sections dealing with employment trends and policies, including the five action points indicated in the European Council's conclusions at Essen.
   - reinforce the co-operative machinery with the appropriate departments of the Member States and in the relevant committees in order to ensure the flow of information necessary for monitoring and assessing Member States progress with respect to these programmes. In particular more frequent and more up to date statistical data on employment and the exchange of information on experiences and 'best practices' should be considered.
   - ensure the coherence between the Structural Funds and the individual Member State multi-annual programmes, paying particular attention to the implementation of the Community Support Frameworks and Community Initiatives.

7. As a first step the Commission will include a larger and more developed employment chapter in its

recommendation for the 'broad guidelines' for the economic policies of the Member States and of the Community, starting in the spring of 1995. The Commission's annual Employment Report will be focused this year on the five key areas concerning employment and training systems identified in Essen and will be presented before the summer.

8. The Commission will present, at the beginning of October of each year, an overview document on employment trends and on the development of employment systems as defined in the White Paper. The Community institutions, in particular the European Parliament, and the Social Partners would be invited to examine it and to give their opinions.

   This document would concentrate on progress in creating jobs, in reducing unemployment — especially among young people and the long term unemployed — in increasing the employment content of growth and in improving the functioning of Member State employment systems. In this context, particular attention will be paid to trends and developments in the education and training fields. The document will assess macro-economic and structural policies affecting the labour market as well as policies towards human resources, training, equal opportunities, local development, small and medium-sized enterprises and the labour market.

   The document which will be presented in October 1995 will contain an initial assessment of the five action points adopted at Essen and specific sections dealing with the two issues which the Essen European Council identified as requiring particular policy attention: the effects of tax and income support systems on the readiness both to create and to take up jobs, and the inter-relationship between economic growth and the environment.

9. The Commission would then report in December to the European Council on the basis of further examination of the above document, taking account of the opinions expressed and incorporating the latest information.

10. Taking into account the October document provided by the Commission, the Social Affairs and the Economic and

Financial Affairs Councils may wish to transmit to the European Council a joint report on these questions.

11. In order to contribute to the coherent approach outlined above, the Commission wishes to further encourage the Social Dialogue at Member State and Community levels and welcomes the initiative of the French Presidency to hold a high level conference in Paris in March 1995.

The Commission wishes equally to see the role of the Standing Committee for Employment developed in the process and recalls that, as stated in its White Paper on Social Policy, it will be presenting proposals this year with a view to improving the role and functioning of the Standing Committee.

Conclusion

12. The Commission seeks the agreement of the Council to the approach set out in this Communication, so that all necessary steps can be taken to ensure a well-co-ordinated process throughout the year which could be endorsed by the European Council in Cannes in June.

Surveillance procedures in the first half of the year

The Commission adopts and publishes the Annual Economic Report

Opinion of the European Parliament	Opinion of the Committee of the Regions	Opinion of the Economic and Social Committee	Opinion(s) of the social partners	Other contributions

The Commission adopts its recommendation for the guidelines

The Monetary Committee prepares the Council discussion

The EcoFin Council "formulates" the draft guidelines

The European Council "discusses a conclusion on the guidelines"

The EcoFin Council adopts the Broad Guidelines

The Council informs the European Parliament

Surveillance procedures in the second half of the year

The Commission adopts and publishes the Employment Report

The Commission adopts its "overview" report

Opinion of the European Parliament

Opinion of the Committee of the Regions

Opinion of the Economic and Social Committee

Opinion(s) of the social partners

Standing Employment Committee

The Social Affairs Council examines the overview report of the Commission

The EcoFin Council examines the overview report of the Commission

The Commission reports to the European Council taking into account the opinions expressed

The European Council assesses progress in creating jobs and reducing unemployment

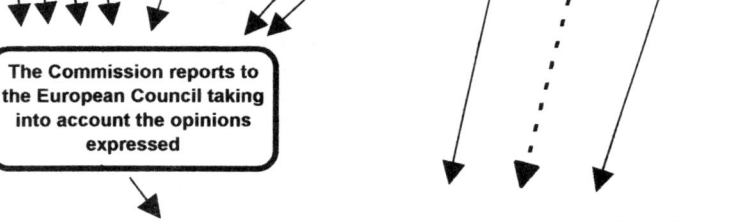

PART IV

The Two Reports
for the Committee

CHAPTER 14

Action Plan:
the First Report

The resolution on an action plan on employment policy to be adopted at the Essen European Council meeting of 9th-10th December 1994, was considered by the European Parliament on December 1st 1994 and was agreed with 268 votes for, 10 against, and 30 abstentions.

— having regard to the Treaty establishing the European Community, particularly Articles 2, 3a, 103(2) and 118 thereof,

— having regard to Rule 135 of its Rules of Procedure,

— having regard to its decision of 20 July 1994 on the setting up, number of members, mandate, powers and responsibilities of a temporary committee on employment,[1] particularly paragraph 2, third subparagraph thereof,

— having regard to the decisions of the European Council at its meetings at Edinburgh, Copenhagen, Brussels and Corfu,

— having regard to the White Paper on Growth, Competitiveness and Employment (COM(93)0700) and the Commission Report — Employment in Europe 1994 (COM(94)0381),

— having regard to its resolutions of 2 December 1993 on the broad guidelines of the economic policies of the Member States and of the Community,[2] 9 March 1994 on the Commission White Paper on Growth, Competitiveness and Employment[3] and 10 March 1994 on employment in Europe,[4]

— having regard to the report of its Temporary Committee on Employment and to the opinion of the Committee on Economic and Monetary Affairs and Industrial Policy (A4-0056/94),

A. whereas high unemployment, low employment rates and regional disparities are problems facing all Member States; whereas common and joint policies agreed at Union level which take full account of the needs of economic and social cohesion need to be developed, and Member State measures in this area coordinated, in order to tackle these problems,

B. whereas the right to work is an inalienable right for every European citizen and must be enshrined in the future Constitution of the Union,

C. whereas the question of employment must be seen in the context of the globalization of the economy; whereas a constructive dialogue is needed at world level,

D. whereas the current level of unemployment in the European Union represents a huge and unacceptable cost in economic and human terms which is undermining the Union's social fabric,

E. whereas despite the relatively high economic level of the Union the number of people living under the poverty line is still on the increase,

F. whereas the White Paper on Growth, Competitiveness and Employment set out a medium term strategy for the Union and its Member States with the aim of creating fifteen million sustainable new jobs; whereas this White Paper was endorsed by the Brussels European Council meeting in December 1993 on the basis of which the European Council adopted an action plan,

G. whereas the jobs created by growth are available to workers with good qualifications, whilst those destroyed by increased competitiveness are unskilled jobs or inappropriately skilled, so that this situation necessarily results in a constant increase in long-term unemployment, causing social exclusion among the most vulnerable groups — women, workers over the age of 50, the disabled, and young people without training,

H. whereas the European Council decided in Corfu that a new action plan would be adopted at its meeting in Essen in December 1994; whereas only through the involvement of the European Parliament in the drawing up of this plan will its institutional legitimacy and public acceptance be ensured,

I
GENERAL PRINCIPLES

1. Reaffirms its view that the problem of unemployment in the European Union is a major challenge which it must tackle and that the objective of creating at least fifteen million sustainable new jobs by the turn of the century should be an overriding priority;

2. Believes that while sustainable economic growth in the Union is a necessary condition for creating new jobs it is not a sufficient one, and accepts, in addition, that the Union must pursue structural reforms as set out below in order to convert economic growth into more jobs;

3. Believes this is the more urgent since new technologies and methods of work organization may not only reinforce competitiveness in many firms and create new jobs, but also reduce employment in the short term in others; asserts, accordingly, that the jobs created by growth are not of the same type as those destroyed only by increased productivity; although growth may help to reduce some kinds of unemployment, it will have no impact on the long-term unemployment which causes exclusion; it must not be used as a pretext for backpedalling on measures to combat social exclusion, but as a means of strengthening those measures;

4. Recognizes that the economic success of the EU is linked to global trade; recognizes that poverty and indebtedness in developing countries has a serious impact on the EU's ability to export goods and to create employment in Member States; in order to achieve that objective, policies of support for the developing countries must be developed and there is also a need to incorporate into international trade agreements and put forward for adoption by the new World Trade Organization (WTO) an environmental clause and a social clause which is based on compliance with the conventions of the International Labour Organization (ILO) and which includes, as a minimum, rules on child labour, the right of association and the prohibition of forced labour;

5. Maintains that more effective structural policies are

needed to create employment, and that these actions should be accompanied by active participation of the social partners and given adequate financial backing, particularly that based on private/public partnerships; confirms the need to develop the social dialogue, as outlined in the Maastricht protocol, since this is essential for carrying out successfully the measures needed to create jobs;

6. Considers that monetary, currency and financial coordination at EU level is important notably from the point of view of employment policy; stresses that exceptionally large increases in long-term interest rates at the beginning of a cyclical upswing have an adverse effect on investment decisions and calls for a marked reduction in base rates to check an interest rate increase in the capital markets; to this end, a coordinated policy on the part of the central banks would be desirable; criticises the lack of transparency and social legitimation of the monetary institutions whose decisions have an impact on financial and wage policy;

7. Agrees with the recommendation made by the European Council in Edinburgh that the Community and the Member States must make sustained efforts to promote clean technologies and non-polluting industrial products and production processes, as well as the objective of 'environmentally sustainable development' proposed by Parliament in its resolution of 7 April 1992 on the results of the intergovernmental conferences;[5] believes that Europe's future competitiveness will be secured only if European governments and institutions rally to the challenge of environmentally, socially and economically sustainable development and would welcome the development of an action programme based on Chapter 10 of the White Paper;

8. Expects the Council not to seek the solution to the problem of unemployment in the systematic dismantling of social security or job protection, but urges the Council, the Commission and the Member States to introduce a programme of economic renewal in their respective spheres of competence based on the following principles:

better economic and monetary cooperation among the Member States to safeguard the attainment of the internal market and restore the credibility of monetary union, removal of the remaining obstacles to the completion of the internal market in order to make the European economy more competitive, a better balance between taxation on work and on capital and the environment, improved support for small and medium-sized enterprises (SMEs) in the form of legislation and tax arrangements which benefit new businesses in particular and stimulate the creation of new jobs, research and development funding at the same level as in other industrialized countries, more productive investment and a more active trade policy;

9. Reaffirms its attachment to the European social model which seeks not only an efficiently functioning market which takes account of the requirements of sustainable development, but also a high level of employment and effective social protection, and considers that, by setting political and social objectives directed towards a new model of development based on these criteria, the Member States will help Europe's citizens to find the confidence needed to overcome the crisis;

II
IMPLEMENTATION OF THE WHITE PAPER

10. Reaffirms its support for the medium-term strategy set out in the White Paper on Growth, Competitiveness and Employment, which combines the essential elements for the Union to escape from its unemployment malaise, and would resist any attempts to undermine that strategy; believes that all policies should continue to be monitored as to their actual or likely impact on competitiveness, economic growth and employment; believes that despite the signs of economic upswing, there is still insufficient demand and insufficient resources to achieve the White Paper's objective of creating fifteen million jobs by the end of the century;

11. Considers that the environmental impact of infrastructure network projects should always be carefully assessed and

monitored, in accordance with the provisions of the ESPOO Convention, of which the European Community is a full member;

12. Refers to the Structural Funds, the Cohesion Fund and the lending facility under the European Investment Fund (EIF) and looks to the Member States to use the financial resources that are available in an efficient manner to create new jobs and activities and to coordinate effectively the measures that are funded in this way; understands the difficulties which faced the Council in setting the borrowing limits for the EIF; is nevertheless concerned that its ECU 8 billion borrowing limit is below what is required to meet the employment objectives of the White Paper; believes that the EIF must be endowed with more resources without endangering policies to attain the Maastricht convergence criteria;

13. Is also concerned that this decision nullifies the instrument through which infrastructural and other investment needed for economic and social cohesion could be combined with observance of the Maastricht convergence criteria; points out that, in order to avoid international capital market trends with an adverse impact on employment, a consistent policy of stability and a solid budgetary policy should be implemented; asks for EU diplomatic action for a new international monetary agreement;

III
A NEW EMPLOYMENT ACTION PLAN FOR ESSEN
a) Member State actions

14. Affirms that the seven areas of labour market policy agreed at Brussels should continue to form a general framework for Member State actions; considers that in the seven areas agreed on in Brussels a short-term priority is the qualification of workers to enable them to adapt to economic and technological changes and reduce the risk of unemployment; believes, also, that in addition to the seven areas others should also be stressed, notably policies to improve the business environment for SMEs, measures concerning the organization of working time,

long-term unemployment and investment in human resources: education, training, continuing training and the acquisition of professional qualifications; stresses the importance of education, vocational training and continuous and further education as a key to improving employment opportunities;

15. Believes that Member States still need to do more to reduce labour costs, specifically non-wage labour costs, particularly at the unskilled end of the labour market where such costs are disproportionately high, by shifting the burden of taxation and employers' contributions so that current levels of social protection are not reduced; calls for a European blueprint for an alternative scheme for financing non-wage labour costs for less-qualified jobs; where appropriate, differentiation by sector may be agreed between the two sides of industry;

16. Believes at the same time, however, that social protection and tax systems must function so that incentives to work are maintained and incentives for the black economy discouraged; also believes that public spending must be used rationally and therefore abuses in the supply of public services, clandestine work and illegal employment have to be combated efficiently;

17. Believes that such shifts may be sought via a fiscal policy — rightly mentioned in the White Paper on growth, competitiveness and employment — which would shift the tax burden from labour to factors such as the environment, natural resources and energy; takes the view that new sources of finance for social protection must be tapped in order to reduce the burden of non-wage labour costs;

18. Is convinced that there is great scope in Member States for job creation in a number of emerging employment areas, especially in the health and other caring services, the environmental, leisure, tourism, craft and cultural sectors, ecological farming, business, trade and audiovisual services as well as encouraging new initiatives including the establishment of "service vouchers" as outlined in the White Paper; believes that giving higher priority to such areas of employment will in turn generate

other jobs in both the public and private sectors, even in areas which have traditionally been situated within the public sector;

19. Stresses the importance of ensuring that the new Community initiatives are implemented without delay and draws particular attention to the job creation potential of the initiatives for SMEs, LEADER and URBAN;

20. Recognizes that many of the new jobs needed in the Union, including those mentioned above, can be created by SMEs; takes the view, however, that Member States need to do more to improve the business environment for SMEs by simplifying regulations, ensuring a more favourable fiscal treatment and facilitating their access to public procurement markets and to new technologies; a reduced VAT rate on labour-intensive services e.g. by expanding Annex H of Directive 92/77/EEC[6] would be a particularly welcome measure;

21. Reiterates its view that positive flexibility within the labour market, particularly as regards working time and work organization, can help to meet the needs of both employers and employees; stresses that more flexible work patterns must be accompanied by supporting measures with regard, for example, to childcare and equivalent levels of protection; strongly urges that directives concerning secondment of employees, parental leave and part-time, temporary and interim work should be adopted as a matter of priority;

22. Notes that according to the new Employment in Europe Report almost nine million workers in the Union work on average more that 48 hours a week and believes that there exists scope for creating jobs if average working time could be reduced; is convinced that by distributing the work available among more people, an important contribution would be made to job creation and lowering the number of redundancies; calls on the social partners, the Member States and the Union to take steps to encourage part-time work, career breaks, training leave, sabbaticals and other ways of reducing working time, while ensuring that the competitiveness of businesses and the social protection of workers are not jeopardized in the process;

23. Views with concern the imbalance between the demand and supply for skilled labour; urges Member States to develop their initial and continuing training systems and to ensure these systems are able to adapt to changes in the labour market;

24. Takes the view that, since they play a decisive role in the creation of new jobs, local authorities must be assessed as to their ability to create new employment in their areas; it is also desirable that in promoting local development the relevant bodies should consult the social partners on a permanent basis to encourage greater cooperation and participation in the decisions on action to be taken;

25. Believes that the European Union and the Member States should create the conditions to guarantee young people access to work or appropriate, efficient and recognized vocational training schemes and notes that a wide range of training courses and measures with different requirements are needed and that all young people who wish to do so should have the opportunity of improving their vocational qualifications and adjusting to changes due to technological progress; looks therefore to the Council to implement as soon as possible the Leonardo and Socrates programmes as approved by the European Parliament, and calls on the Member States to prioritize actions aimed at young people who are particularly vulnerable to unemployment; calls on the Commission to act upon the proposals for a programme as put forward in the White Paper;

26. Calls on the Member States to develop actively the social and labour market infrastructure in order to respond positively to changing gender roles in society, and in particular to identify gender-related barriers relating to childcare, taxation, social security and labour regulation issues (for example, take action to individualize tax/social security arrangements);

27. Points out that under no circumstances may the principle of equal labour market opportunities and equal treatment of men and women or the policy of equal opportunities be violated;

28. Calls for further positive actions to integrate people with a disability into the labour market;

b) Actions to be undertaken by the Union

29. Is convinced that labour costs must be brought down, particularly at the lower end of the labour market; points out in this context that the important step of reducing non-wage labour costs in the Member States is dependent upon the adoption at European level of compensatory measures, particularly environmental, consumer and property taxes; calls on the Council to honour its obligations in this respect;

30. Believes that Member States should develop clear strategies both within and across Member States, to implement the objectives of the above and other agreed areas of labour market policy and local development strategies; believes that social and economic criteria, which reflect diverse approaches and problems, should be established to measure progress, with appropriate statistical tools, of Member State policies on the basis of a regular reporting procedure; Member State actions should be complemented by accompanying actions undertaken by the Commission where these can add value to national policies;

31. Calls on the European Council, in implementation of Chapter 10 of the White Paper and by analogy with its initiatives in the areas of trans-European networks and the information society, to take steps to create new jobs in the framework of a social model based on sustainable development and designed to improve the quality of life and the chances of employment for everyone in the European Union, particularly women; requests the European Council to instruct the Commission to draw up an action programme, including proposals on financing and the environment, in this context;

32. Notes also that Article 103(2) of the EC Treaty determines that 'The Council shall, acting by a qualified majority on a recommendation from the Commission, formulate a draft for the broad guidelines of the economic policies of the Member States and of the Community'; urges the Commission to give priority to the formulation of new guidelines focused on employment creation in the context of the economic upturn;

33. Calls for measures to strengthen economic and social cohesion in the European Union and to buttress genuine convergence efforts in its less-developed Member States; asks the Council to convince the Member States that structural fund resources are fully and properly utilized and that they are used in the interests of both economic and social cohesion;

34. Calls on the Council and Commission to devise a European accounting mechanism to provide a global picture of the European economy and common economic aggregates permitting effective coordination of the Member States' economic policies;

35. Urges appropriate increases in the borrowing limits of the European Union and/or European Investment Fund to enable appropriate finance in trans-European infrastructure projects and urges the establishment of public/ private partnerships to finance these projects; considers that the EIF must be able to intervene to assist SMEs, to allow guarantee consortiums to be set up to provide access to credit, with a view to promoting and supporting the development of real services for SMEs and so as to encourage the decentralization of instruments giving shareholders access to the market; urges the European Council at Essen to endorse these proposals as a major dimension of the activities of an expanded EIF;

36. Calls for better coordination of economic policy in the EU and reforms in research and development cooperation so as to allow the European dimension of industrial policy to take effect; calls for rapid decision-taking in the field of industrial policy and an initiative at EU level to implement a framework which fosters industrial innovation, notably in the field of data-processing;

37. Stresses the importance of EURES and other European initiatives aimed at creating a cross-border labour market, particularly in frontier areas with a (potentially) high level of labour mobility; points in this context to the many obstacles which still stand in the way of cross-border labour mobility, particularly the fiscal penalties attached to cross-border work;

c) **Monitoring and follow-up procedures**

38. Urgently requests the Council to assist the Commission to include in the coming work programme, and in subsequent annual work programmes, a detailed statement of the planned increases in employment overall, and an account of the funding provisions which will underpin them;

39. Suggests that overall monitoring of the action plan be undertaken by the Commission in conjunction with the Social Affairs and ECOFIN Councils, and that the Commission present on a half-yearly basis a progress report on the implementation of the action plan to the European Council, the European Parliament and the Economic and Social Committee and the social partners;

40. Mandates its President to present the following declaration of the European Parliament to the European Council meeting in Essen:

> *'There can be no more important priority than the implementation of the White Paper.*
>
> *The 15 million new jobs, as agreed by the Council, Commission and European Parliament, will only be created if the European Union and its Member States make the following commitments:*
>
> — *to use the present recovery to create sustainable growth and employment and to reaffirm and implement the strategies set out in the White Paper,*
>
> — *to strengthen and develop the EIF or other appropriate instruments in order to mobilise private and public investment so as to improve production capacity and enhance economic and social infrastructure; invites the Council to present a concrete plan for financing the investments defined in the White Paper,*
>
> — *to create positive flexibility by developing an active employment policy, supplemented by a determined effort to get those in the greatest difficulty back to work, based on substantial investment in human resources for a high skilled and adaptive society; invites the Council to set targets for common efforts*

in the Member States,

— *to strengthen the policies and programmes to combat youth and long-term unemployment, and to integrate the disabled and the socially excluded into the labour market; expects the Council to come back to Parliament with adequate proposals,*

— *to transform the present economy into one which is more sustainable by designing reforms in taxation with a view to achieving greater balance, taking account of the protection of the environment; expects the Council to give the Commission a mandate to negotiate proposals for substantial improvements before the end of the decade,*

— *to support an initiative for new policies to stabilise financial markets and to demand improved coordination of different policies.*

We cannot afford to fail our peoples in this promise.

The States and Institutions of our Europe will be measured by their success in facing this challenge.'

41. Instructs its President to forward this resolution to the European Council, Council, Commission, Economic and Social Committee and Governments of the Member States.

References

1. OJ C 261, 19.9.1994, p.27.
2. OJ C 342, 20.12.1993, p.23.
3. OJ C 91, 28.03.1994, p.124.
4. OJ C 91, 28.03.1994, p.224.
5. OJ C 125, 18.5.1992, p.81.
6. OJ L 316, 31.10.1992, p.1.

CHAPTER 15

The Employment Committee's Final Report

The resolution on a coherent employment strategy for the European Union was debated on July 12th, 1995, at the Plenary Session in Strasbourg. The vote the following day gave it an overwhelming majority of 234 to 88, with 31 abstentions.

K.C.

The European Parliament,

— having regard to the Treaty establishing the European Community, particularly Articles 2, 3a, 103(2) and 118 thereof,

— having regard to Rule 135 of its Rules of Procedure,

— having regard to its decision of 20 July 1994 on the setting up, number of members, mandate, powers and responsibilities of a temporary committee on employment,[1] particularly paragraph 2, third subparagraph thereof,

— having regard to the decisions of the European Council at its meetings at Edinburgh, Copenhagen, Brussels, Corfu, Essen and Cannes,

— having regard to the White Paper on Growth, Competitiveness and Employment (COM(93)0700),

— having regard to the Commission report 'Employment in Europe 1994' (COM(94)0381),

— having regard to the Communication from the Commission to the Council on the Follow-up to the Essen European Council on Employment (COM(95)0074),

— having regard to its resolutions of 9 March 1994 on the Commission White Paper on Growth, Competitiveness and Employment,[2] 10 March 1994 on employment in Europe,[3] 1 December 1994 on an action plan on employment policy to be adopted at the Essen European Council meeting of 9-10 December 1994[4] and of 7 April 1995 on the Commission's Annual Economic Report for 1995 and the Council's report on the implementation of the broad economic policy guidelines,[5]

— having regard to the report of the International Labour Office on world employment 1995, which recognizes that high levels of unemployment spawn a host of problems including a growing inequality and social exclusion, increasing economic insecurity and human suffering, and which concludes that there would be 'vast benefits from a renewed commitment by all nations to the objective of full employment',

— taking into account the Joint Opinion drawn up by the Macroeconomic Group of the Social Dialogue under the title 'The Social Partners' Guidelines for Turning Recovery into a Sustained and Job-Creating Growth Process' of 16 May 1995, signed by the European Trade Unions Confederation (ETUC), the Union of Industrial and Employers' Confederation of Europe (UNICE) and the Centre of Enterprises with Public Participation (ECPE),

— having regard to the report of its Temporary Committee on Employment and to the opinions of the Committee on Economic and Monetary Affairs and Industrial Policy, the Committee on Social Affairs and Employment and the Committee on Regional Policy (A4-0166/95),

A. whereas the White Paper on Growth, Competitiveness and Employment put forward proposals the objective of which was to create 15 million new jobs in the European Union by the end of the century,

B. whereas the European Union must remain committed to this objective if it is not to lose the confidence of its citizens; whereas failure would risk undermining popular support for the goal of European integration itself,

C. whereas the fight against social exclusion which takes into account the unemployed and in particular the long-term unemployed must be addressed as a top priority by national measures and Community actions including the

Structural Funds, the new Community initiatives and the Fourth Poverty Programme,

D. whereas economic and monetary union will in time create a more stable economic environment and facilitate action to create employment but progress towards it will require further action to assist job creation and ensure social cohesion,

E. whereas restoring a high level of employment is one of the means of reducing debt and annual deficits by reducing unemployment compensation and generating direct and indirect tax revenues from those newly in work,

F. whereas net achievement of the fifteen million jobs target of the White Paper on Growth, Competitiveness and Employment requires that the European Union adopt a coherent employment strategy which must be based first and foremost on the recognition that the efforts of the European Union, Member States, regional and local authorities and social partners need to combine effective measures at each appropriate level; whereas financial policy co-ordination will without doubt be an important means of achieving this,

G. whereas employment strategies demand that policy be directed not only at carrying out structural reforms designed to enhance job-creation as a direct consequence of economic growth but also at ensuring that such growth is sustainable, environment-friendly and increases the competitiveness of the European economy,

H. having regard to the increase in the number of decisions to restructure, relocate and close transnational undertakings, causing not only a general decline in employment but also a climate of growing uncertainty among workers and the public as a whole,

I. underlining the importance of education and training as an integral part of employment policy and welcoming recent Council decisions in this field,

J. whereas, with due regard for the different levels of responsibility in this area, employment strategies need to be accompanied by a monitoring, co-ordination and co-operation procedure in which performance is measured against agreed criteria, such a procedure being conducted in the most transparent manner possible,

K.   whereas the decisions taken at the Essen European Council concentrate on certain aspects of structural reform; whereas, however, they are far too timid and fall short of implementing the employment strategy which had already been agreed for the European Union, which should not only make progress with the trans-European networks, but also provide European investment aid to small and medium enterprises within the framework of a balanced regional policy,

L.   whereas these earlier decisions need to be supplemented, as do the Essen decisions, particularly as regards the role of the European Union, and its institutions in investment and employment policy, the growth aspects of job creation and the establishment of a monitoring procedure by which Member State actions can be evaluated,

I. POLICIES

1.   Believes that the objective of the White Paper on Growth, Competitiveness and Employment, of creating 15 million new, long-term jobs, to halve the rate of unemployment, must be one of the greatest priorities for the Union, the Member States, regional and local authorities and the social partners, and that continuing mass unemployment threatens social and economic cohesion, acceptance and progress to further European integration and the future of the democratic system;

2.   Calls on the European Council and Commission to incorporate the right to work in the Treaty when it is revised at the 1996 Intergovernmental Conference;

3.   Believes that a coherent strategy for employment must mean that all policies having an impact on employment, namely economic, financial, structural, environmental, industrial, commercial and social, are integrated into an overarching policy dedicated to job creation; urges the European Union and Member States to carry out such an integrated approach and to ensure that the strategies of each are complementary to one another; nevertheless,

while such an integrated approach must be stressed, sets out below policy areas it considers as having priority;

4. Notes that the Community gives extensive financial support to socio-economic development through its Structural Funds, Cohesion Fund and Community Initiatives and insists that these funds be incorporated by Member States and the Community in an effective and co-ordinated fashion into their employment strategies with special reference being given to different target groups facing particular difficulties in finding or developing employment opportunities as well as SMEs and local economic actors;

5. Calls on the Commission and Council to endeavour to implement the policy of major infrastructure projects which will be a new departure for European integration and the fight against unemployment; deplores the successive failures of the Essen and Cannes summits in this area;

6. Believes that a coherent employment strategy must emphasize equality between men and women; the difficulties which women face in finding work currently constitute an enormous problem on which particular attention will be focused; equality in paid and non-paid working time must be considered as an integral part of such a policy;

7. Calls on the Commission to endeavour to introduce social legislation in accordance with the French Presidency's memorandum in the World Trade Organization; calls on the Commission to apply the arrangements suspending the Community's system of generalized preference with regard to the practice of any form of forced labour and the export of products manufactured in prisons;

8. Calls on the Commission and the Member States to urge Community-scale undertakings to refrain from taking decisions which have adverse effects on employment, of which workers have not previously been informed, on which no prior consultation has taken place and which are not accompanied by a credible retraining plan in accordance with the aim of Directive 94/45/EC,[6]

a) Macroeconomic policy

9. Recognizes that the fulfilment of the convergence criteria laid down in the Treaty on European Union requires that the Member States pursue sound budgetary and monetary policies; expects that this will create a more stable economic climate and so help boost investment and employment; believes, however, that progress to economic and monetary union needs to be balanced with an active employment strategy and that this will require additional, Union level, financial instruments capable of meeting investment and job-creation objectives; compliments the European Council, therefore, on its foresight in agreeing to the establishment of the EIF and Union Bonds and urges that these instruments be used in the most effective and efficient way possible and, where necessary, they be expanded so as to maintain public and private investment, boost SME development, create jobs and offset the possible deflationary impact of convergence plans;

10. Asks the Commission to carry out an on-going assessment to clarify the correlation of employment policy with the other economic policies, in particular monetary and interest-rate policy, and to ascertain how these policies can help to maintain a high level of activity and hence a low level of unemployment;

11. Believes that policies designed to maintain and increase both growth and investment in human and physical capital should, inter alia, make provision for a doubling of expenditure on R&D, thereby bringing Europe into line with the economic areas which are in direct competition with the European Union; such policies should aim at a spending target of 3 per cent of European Union GDP to be dedicated to R&D not later than the year 2000;

12. Notes the findings of the Commission's 1995 Annual Economic Report and its conclusion that growth can be sustained in the European economy until the year 2000; nevertheless, requests that the Commission publish its own estimates of both the potential deflationary effects of fulfilling the financial convergence criteria and the

feasibility of offsetting this through expansion of the borrowing and lending facilities of Union Bonds and the European Investment Fund;

b) *Reduction of working time*
   and new methods of work organization

13. Recognizes that investments and economic growth alone will not be sufficient to achieve the fifteen million jobs target but considers that, among other measures, a better distribution of available work should contribute to a solution in the short term;

14. Believes that, while systems of leave for family, personal or training reasons, the encouragement of part-time working and reductions in working time, whether their effects are felt in days, weeks, years or in the course of a lifetime, are not the only solution, they always offer a possible way of dovetailing supply and demand in the labour market more closely and satisfying people's wish for a better quality of life and greater freedom to organize their own time;

15. Considers that the example of firms engaging in negotiations with their staff for a reduction of working time confirms the effectiveness of this approach in terms of employment and job creation, but notes that this practice is not advancing quickly enough to contribute to the overall solution to the problem; considers that this lack of progress is also due to a combination of factors — disregarding qualitative drawbacks — namely, that employers cannot afford higher unit costs, which would jeopardize their competitiveness, and that employees, particularly those in the modest income groups, cannot afford to lose a substantial part of their income without any compensatory wage adjustment;

16. Considers, therefore, that the project of reducing working hours would be facilitated by the establishment of a system of direct or indirect aid, intended either to pay for new recruitment or to offset wage reductions, with priority given to modest wage-earners; believes that in most Member States this aid could be funded from the savings

made in spending on unemployment assistance whenever an unemployed person covered by them entered employment; Member States can allow these funds to be reallocated, but must not in any circumstances lay down precise rules governing either the reduction of working time or partial or total compensatory wage adjustments, which must be contractually negotiated by the social partners;

17. Calls on the Commission to invite the social partners and report on the impact of the Directive concerning certain aspects of working time which is due to be implemented in all Member States by 23 November 1996; calls on the Commission, further, to continue its discussions with the social partners and/or studies on the activities or sectors excluded from the Directive;

18. Is convinced that the introduction of a variety of leave arrangements for family, personal or training reasons would answer people's need to combine their work, social and family lives more effectively; is convinced that these arrangements would increase the flexibility of work management and that career breaks of this kind would create job opportunities for the unemployed people recruited in their place; calls accordingly on the social partners to conclude an agreement in this area at European level;

19. Considers that the internal flexibility of undertakings and work organization cannot be improved without taking into account the specific situation of each production sector and each undertaking; considers that this must reflect the need to improve the quality of life; considers, therefore, that the social partners must play a crucial role in the process of change, by means of negotiation and consensus rather than imposed solutions;

20. Calls on the social partners, the Member States and the Union to take measures to promote part-time work, reduction in annual and life working time, the interruption of professional activity, paid leave for vocational training and other forms of reduction in working time, while ensuring that these measures do not jeopardize the

competitiveness of undertakings or the social protection of employees and that services on which employees are dependent are provided;

21. Warns against exaggerated hopes that reduced working time can be translated entirely into a reduction of unemployment, since some of the resulting labour supply will not be matched by corresponding demand, and calls in addition for specific efforts to achieve the best possible translation of reduced working time into the creation and filling of new jobs;

22. Calls on the Commission to submit as a priority a report on the possible trade-off between early retirement and recruitment of the long-term unemployed;

23. Recommends that the adoption of new and more flexible work practices and adaptation to new methods of work organization be promoted within the terms of reference of the new Objective 4 of the Structural Funds and the ADAPT Initiative so as to improve efficiency and develop human resources; considers, however, that moves to make the organization of work more flexible should be accompanied by corresponding new regulations governing the labour market, set if necessary at the European level, so as to avoid the risks of social dumping and that the introduction of flexible work practices be the subject of agreement between the social partners;

24. Reiterates its view that labour market deregulation is not in itself a means to create new jobs and must on no account lead to an increase in the numbers of 'second-class jobs' characterized by very low wages, poor working conditions, lack of security, and limited benefits;

25. Believes that labour market flexibility defined in terms of adaptability and readiness to adopt new work patterns or methods of work organization can benefit both employees and employers and is an important factor for ensuring that European enterprises remain competitive and that human resources are most effective;

26. Reiterates its call for European measures to facilitate cross-border job mobility, particularly in border areas, by

the removal of the many remaining obstacles particularly in the areas of taxation, social security and access to social services and health care, and calls for the introduction of a 'European assessment' to ascertain the impact of planned national measures on cross-border migration of workers within the Union;

c) *New employment areas*
   and raising the employment content of jobs

27. Believes that the European Council at Essen was right to recommend to Member States that initiatives should be promoted to create jobs which take account of new requirements; takes the view that there is great potential for new employment in the field of professional services in the personal, family, social, cultural, tourism, leisure and especially environmental sectors but that, for this to be achieved, Member States have to engage in, and the European Union has to encourage, imaginative policy choices; in particular stresses that the Member States must implement policies, especially fiscal policies, designed both to encourage private demand to shift towards social, cultural and environmental assets and to stimulate supply, by promoting partnership between the public and private sectors and encouraging initiatives by co-operatives and voluntary organizations; this would make it possible to pursue simultaneously the objective of improving the efficiency and quality of social, cultural and environmental services and promoting employment;

28. Calls on the Commission, on the basis of research and enquiries already carried out, to submit a comprehensive report on experience gained in this field in the different countries, also formulating proposals and suggestions on ways and means which may usefully be applied, in the Union and in the Member States, for developing these new areas for economic and social initiatives;

29. Points out that productivity or economic viability in sectors such as education, health or social services cannot be measured according to the same criteria as productivity or viability in other production sectors, although these

sectors can be managed effectively in such a way as to develop their potential for job creation and at the same time improve the quality of the service;

30. Points out that, despite the low level of funding provided for the three Poverty Programmes, some success was achieved in the creation of employment and accordingly renews its call on the Council to finally adopt the Poverty Four Programme in order to reinforce solidarity with the most disadvantaged groups in society;

31. Considers that the development of a sector geared to regional and social requirements, as a third sector between the trade-oriented private sector and the public sector, organized primarily on the basis of socially beneficial organizations and co-operatives, constitutes an important task for the future;

32. Takes the view that there is also job-creating and job-saving potential to be exploited through the application of new information technologies so long as these technologies are used judiciously in all their applications in the private, non-profit and public sectors in a way which increases opportunities and choices for all citizens and not only a privileged minority;

33. Urges that, in order to assist Member State policy development, the Commission in conjunction with relevant Councils organize fora in which exchanges of ideas, initiatives and good practice in the field of new employment areas can take place and proposes that the Council should provide appropriate funding for Member States' projects in this field;

d) *SMEs*

34. Is convinced that SMEs, and in particular very small and micro-sized enterprises, have the greatest job creating potential of all enterprise types; notes that the Essen recommendations have across the board relevance for SMEs; recommends to Member States that in implementing their multi-annual programmes in the areas identified in the Essen decisions that they pay particular attention to the needs and interests of SMEs;

35. Insists that support be given for the economic development of SMEs in general, and in particular those SMEs which are innovative, which export, invest, recruit and train staff and whose activities are compatible with the environment; urges that this be done by creating a proper fiscal, social, administrative and legal framework which encourages good recruitment decisions; notes in this connection the particular importance of the completion of the internal market, inter alia in the field of technical specifications, standardization and certification, of the creation of better funding opportunities, of cross-border co-operation between businesses, of access to public contracts and to Community policies in areas such as research and development, the Structural Funds and the Community initiatives, for both the foundation and the further development of SMEs, and of a stable, transparent and enforceable legal framework and a simplification of bureaucratic procedures. Calls on the Commission to draw up a special programme for SME management training and, in addition, refers to the need for Member States to place more emphasis on entrepreneurial skills;

36. Notes that the high cost of labour especially in the services sector weighs particularly heavily on some SMEs; a reduced VAT rate on labour-intensive services may go some way towards alleviating this burden;

37. Insists on a more active policy by the Union and its financial intermediaries such as the EIB and the EIF to reinforce regional credit institutions in association with regional development agencies in the promotion and reinforcement of local entrepreneurship; this approach may also be used to promote local markets for risk capital (stock exchanges) and to link them to national and European networks;

e) Indirect wage costs

38. Welcomes the idea of fixed-term labour cost contributions for the reintegration of the long-term unemployed in the labour market and the proposals for making public labour

exchanges more efficient in order for them to be more attractive to the employers and to enable job-seekers to be aware of demand for work;

39. Recognizes moreover that private placement agencies may also have a role to play in recruiting people for the jobs available;

40. Calls on the Member States and the two sides of industry to exploit the increase in productivity principally to create additional jobs;

41. Notes that the funding of social security systems can no longer be permitted to represent a damper to employment to the same extent as at present;

42. Considers it would be useful if the European Union carried out a policy of co-ordination *vis-à-vis* the Member States, aimed at a gradual levelling of wage structures as far as taxation is concerned and of contributions, which should be reduced selectively, so as to represent an effective encouragement to recruitment, by devising compensatory taxes such as an environmental tax;

43. Considers that savings on the expenditure side must be accompanied by an attempt to find new sources of funding for social security systems, including compensatory measures to avoid undesirable effects on the distribution of income, in particular for the neediest households and individuals; warns that this must not, however, result in the privatization of social risks; is of the opinion that the financing of social security systems must remain a collective task;

44. Notes that a consensus exists on the need to reduce non-wage labour costs and that some Member States have already taken measures in this area, offsetting public revenue loss by shifting charges and contributions to other sources; believes that the results of these policies should be carefully studied and the findings widely published and distributed;

45. Considers, in view of the development of the internal market, that it is appropriate to carry on discussions at European Union level on alternative sources of funding,

and that the following possibilities currently exist: CO_2 tax, a tax on speculative capital movement, advance levy on investment income and particular VAT rates;

f) *Training and the development of human resources*

46. Points out that vocational training will be attractive only if vocational education provides the basis for lifelong learning and enhances the opportunity to develop an individual's prospects of employment and that it will hold out prospects for the future only if excessively early specialization is avoided, so that trainees do not enter a one-way street leading to an occupation which turns out to have no future;

47. Calls therefore for

—a continuous process of modernization of content and requirements to safeguard and further improve the quality of vocational training and foster creativity and personal commitment,

—the vocational training on offer to be rendered attractive by promoting alternating systems,

—a contribution to be made towards improving the ability of men and women to combine employment with parenthood by making appropriate qualifications available,

—a general improvement in the opportunities for women to participate actively in the economy and in the life of society,

—the integration of training, forms of supplementary qualifications to accompany training, and further training to develop new, *transparent* vocational training which is more coherent in terms of content and times when it can be taken,

—the creation of better career opportunities for employees by introducing permanent education and training systems,

—an improvement in the transparency of further training courses on offer,

—an increase in financial support for further training and an improvement in information on training, promotion and further training prospects,

—an improvement in the training prospects of all young people,

—the option of training for young people who, despite all efforts, do not embark upon vocational training and for adults who have no vocational qualifications,

—special training or further training courses to be provided for older workers, those with health problems and/or the less highly qualified,

—access to a broad vocational spectrum to be ensured during the reorganization of occupations in which training is provided so that the training may prove useful in the long term;

g) Economic democracy

48. Points out that the enhancement of productivity is highly correlated with information, consultation and partici-pation of employees in decision-making in their enterprise, especially where transition to more flexible production methods is concerned; believes that such involvement of employees in the enterprise and at the local, regional, national and EU level should be integral to the new models of economic and social development which must be devised in order to develop sustainability and increase the competitiveness of business in the Union; stresses in this context the importance, in terms of methods and substance, of the document of 16 May 1995 entitled 'The Social Partners — Guidelines for turning the recovery into a sustained and job-creating growth process';

49. Notes the importance of social dialogue at all levels; stresses that the credibility of European SME policy will be seriously jeopardized if the Commission does not take urgent measures to ensure the full participation of SME representatives at all levels of the European social dialogue;

h) Public sector

50. Takes the view that, particularly in view of the challenges posed by ecological restructuring and the new technologies, the redefinition and establishment of a

forward-looking public sector constitutes one of the key political tasks which will be relevant to employment policy, equality between men and women and social protection on society;

II. PROCEDURES

Considers that labour policy and economic policy must not be viewed separately, that co-operation between the Member States and the European Union institutions should be encouraged and that employment should become a central focus of Community policies;

52. Takes note of the Commission's Communication to the Council on the follow-up to the Essen European Council on employment which represents a basis for building a surveillance procedure by which to monitor employment policy and which are a significant response to the ideas set out in paragraphs 30 and 39 of its above-mentioned resolution of 1 December 1994; believes, however, that this is only a first step in the elaboration of a procedure that evaluates the performance of the Member States and the Union in achieving employment and social union;

53. Recommends, in view of the scale of the challenge of achieving both the financial convergence criteria for a single currency and the employment objectives of the White Paper on Growth, Competitiveness and Employment (or, in the words of the Treaty on European Union, 'the objective of a high level of employment and of social protection and the quality of life, and economic and social cohesion and solidarity among Member States'), that the Annual Economic Report and Employment Report should also be submitted to the national and regional parliaments for information and with a view to follow-up;

54. As regards the surveillance procedures in the first half of the year set out in the Commission's Communication proposes that:

—the Commission publish its Annual Economic Report as early as possible in the year and that it include an evaluation of the implementation of the broad economic guidelines adopted the previous year,

—that the initial opinion of the European Parliament should be communicated to national parliaments for them to take into account in their own debates on the report,

—the Social Affairs Ministers be involved in the formulation of the economic guidelines given that these will include a larger and more developed employment chapter,

—the Commission report and discuss its priorities for the economic guidelines before a joint meeting of the Committees on Economic and Monetary Affairs and on Social Affairs and Employment,

—the Commission not adopt its recommendation for the guidelines before Parliament adopts its report on this subject,

—the Council send to Parliament as soon as possible the final text of the guidelines,

—the social partners be involved;

55. As regards the surveillance procedure in the second half of the year,

—urges the Commission to publish its Employment Report in July and its overview report in September,

—expects the Commission to report on and discuss its priorities for the overview report before a joint meeting of the Committees on Social Affairs and Employment and Economic and Monetary Affairs,

—expects the overview report to include an assessment of the Member States employment policies both from an overall point of view and from the point of view of the implementation of Member States multi-annual programmes,

—suggests that the inputs of the Social Affairs and ECOFIN Councils would be made more coherent if those Councils were to hold during this period a joint meeting,

—believes that the Commission's report to the European Council and the conclusions of the European Council itself should take the form of 'employment guidelines' (akin to the economic guidelines) which suggest to Member States improvements to their employment policies in general and their multi-annual programmes in particular,

—proposes that the social partners be involved;

56. Stresses that the Standing Committee on Employment (SCE) should play a prominent role in the new surveillance procedure; hopes that this will be the focus of the new proposal on enhancing the status of the SCE that the Commission has promised in its Medium Term Social Action Programme; states its wish to be represented on the SCE as part of the proposal to enhance its role;

57. Believes that a surveillance procedure must be equipped with measurable criteria to be used to measure performance and where appropriate set targets; suggests that criteria should be related both to employment policy in general as well as to the five action areas established at Essen;

58. Proposes, for the five Essen areas, that Member State policy actions in pursuit of the recommendations and commitments of the European Council should be effectively monitored and assessed and that Member States need to evaluate their actions and demonstrate how specific policy changes are contributing to the achievement of policy goals;

59. Believes that Parliament must be fully involved in the new surveillance procedures in order to ensure that its policy objectives are pursued; instructs, therefore, its two standing committees principally involved with employment policy, the Committee on Social Affairs and Employment and the Committee on Economic and Monetary Affairs and Industrial Policy, along with other standing committees with an interest in employment,

—to draw up for each May plenary session a joint report on the Commission's Annual Economic Report and recommended economic guidelines;

—to draw up for each November plenary session a joint report on the employment overview report;

—in co-operation with all other relevant committees, to

work out the modalities by which the above requirements are organized;

60. Declares that the permanent abolition of unemployment and the achievement of full employment require a degree of social restructuring which goes beyond the recommendations made here; it presupposes radical changes in the whole system of values which impregnate economic life in today's Europe; calls on all those who have faith in humanistic values to join forces for the achievement of the necessary changes;

*   *   *

61. Instructs its President to forward this resolution to the Council, Commission, Economic and Social Committee, the Committee of the Regions and the governments and parliaments of the Member States.

Footnotes

1. OJ C 261, 19.9.1994, p.27.
2. OJ C 91, 28.03.1994, p.124.
3. OJ C 91, 28.03.1994, p.224.
4. OJ C 363, 19.12.1994, p.62.
5. Minutes, of that sitting, Part II, Item 10.
6. OJ L 254, 30.9.1994, p.64.

Elf Books

The Right to Work: The Loss of our First Freedom
compiled and edited by Ken Coates MEP
*with chapters by Michael Barratt Brown, John Hughes
and John Wells*

All over Europe unemployment rages at crisis levels. This remains so,
even if the statistical evidence is sometimes inadequate, even corrupt.
John Wells shows how far the British unemployment statistics are
polluted, while John Hughes reveals a similar level of pollution
among the *employment* statistics. Ken Coates, rapporteur of the
European Parliament's Employment Committee, sets out the efforts
to address unemployment at the European level.

cloth 0 85124 577 3 £30.00 paper 0 85124 578 1 £6.99

The European Recovery Programme: Restoring Full Employment
edited by Ken Coates MEP *& Michael Barratt Brown*

Shorter working time and other changes are crucial to putting Europe
back to work. This volume considers what can be done.

cloth 0 85124 539 0 £30.00 paper 0 85124 549 8 £7.95

Europe Can Afford to Work
by Francis Cripps & Terry Ward

Strategies for growth and employment in the European Community.

cloth 0 85124 551 X £25.00 paper 0 85124 550 1 £4.95

The Evolution of a European: Socialism, Science and Europe
by Glyn Ford MEP

The author's collected writings reveal the close relationship between
science and technology, investment, and industrial society, with
particular reference to Europe and Japan.

cloth 0 85124 560 9 £35.00 paper 0 85124 561 7 £9.99

**Subscription details for *European Labour Forum* journal are
available on request.**

SPOKESMAN

Bertrand Russell House, Gamble Street, Nottingham NG7 4ET. Tel:
(0115) 9708318

Elf Books

The Social Charter and the Single European Market
by John Hughes

With wide-ranging developments and changes set in motion in the course of constructing the single European market, the needs of equity require a rapid evolution of new norms of social and political principle and practice to give substance to the Social Charter.

cloth 0 85124 523 4 £20.00 paper 0 85124 524 2 £6.95

European Union: Fortress or Democracy?
by Michael Barratt Brown

Where is the way forward for economic and political development in the East and the South, as they relate to the whole of Europe, and how are we to overcome the plan-versus-market syndrome?

cloth 0 85124 520 X £20.00 paper 0 85124 521 8 £7.95

Against a Rising Tide: Racism, Europe and 1992
by Mel Read MEP & Alan Simpson MP

How do developments in Europe affect black people in Britain? The authors offer pratical ways in which local people can combat racism, setting their work in a European context.

cloth 0 85124 525 0 £20.00 paper 0 85124 526 9 £6.95

Whatever Happened to the Peace Dividend?
The Post-Cold War Armaments Momentum
by Marek Thee

A new arms race was underway even before the Gulf War. The author sets out the global drive for new high-tech weapons, and makes clear why Europe's arms industry must plan its own conversion.

cloth 0 85124 532 3 £20.00 paper 0 85124 533 1 £7.95

Europe: *an* Ever Closer Union
by David Martin MEP

The European Parliament's main *rapporteur* on polictical union explains the Parliament's strategy for achieving such a union, including re-invigorating democracy through a Europe of the Regions.

cloth 0 8512Y 537 4 £20.00 paper 0 8512Y 538 2 £6.95

Subscription details for *European Labour Forum* journal are available on request.

SPOKESMAN

Bertrand Russell House, Gamble Street, Nottingham NG7 4ET. Tel: (0115) 9708318

THE EUROPEAN IMPERATIVE

Economic and Social Cohesion in the 1990s

by

STUART HOLLAND

"of the first importance . . . deserves to be widely read"

Jacques Delors

1992 was supposed to be the greatest year in the history of the European Community since the signature of the Rome Treaty in 1957. In fact, the result of the first Danish referendum, the strains on the exchange rate mechanism of the EMS, and deepening recession threw it into the biggest crisis since President de Gaulle pulled France out of the Council of Ministers in 1965.

In this report to the EC Commission, Stuart Holland argues that reinforcing the European project is imperative for economic and social progress in its member states. National sovereignty has been eroded by multinational capital, finance and trade. Member states need to act jointly through the Community to achieve objectives such as full employment, rights at work and welfare.

The European Imperative traces arguments relevant to the European Growth Initiative and the European Investment Fund adopted by the Edinburgh European Council in December 1992, and the call by President Mitterrand in October 1993 for a 100 billion ecu borrowing and expenditure programme to modernise the European economy and create employment.

The report argues for policies that can recover investment, income, trade and employment; regenerate industry through new strategies, including Innovation Agreements between the social partners; reduce annual working hours in bigger business and the public sector as a strategy for job creation; reinforce individual and citizenship rights, including the right to negotiate the use of working time; promote regional networking of medium firms to give them some of the features of larger multinationals in international markets; and extend social and regional programmes as a means of promoting both social justice and employment.

£14.95

ISBN 0 85124 558 7

SPOKESMAN, Bertrand Russell House, Gamble Street, Nottingham NG7 4ET. Tel: (0115) 9708318.

European Recovery Programme Essential for Full Employment

A full-blooded European Recovery Programme of joint action by all the states of the European Community is essential to restoring full employment in Europe. It needs to be urged forward by their common institutions, and to emphasize reductions in working time.

In the circumstances of the 1990s, such joint action for economic recovery should naturally be led by the European Commission, and co-ordinated with member governments.

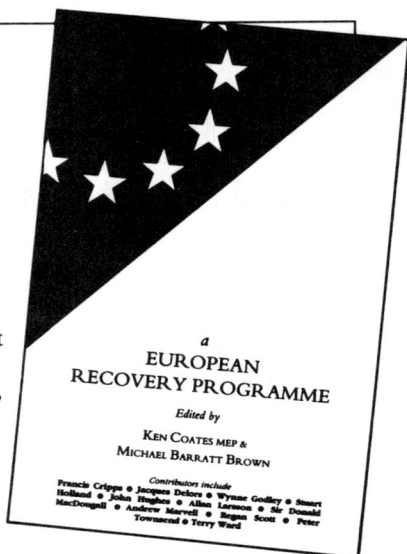

a
EUROPEAN RECOVERY PROGRAMME
Edited by
KEN COATES MEP &
MICHAEL BARRATT BROWN

Contributors include
Francis Cripps • Jacques Delors • Wynne Godley • Stuart Holland • John Hughes • Allan Larsson • Sir Donald MacDougall • Andrew Marvell • Regan Scott • Peter Townsend • Terry Ward

This book proposes a detailed framework for a recovery programme and seeks to prove that mass unemployment is not at all inevitable and can be overcome. It will be of interest to trade unionists and all those concerned with the crisis in employment and social provision.

A European Recovery Programme: Restoring Full Employment, edited by Ken Coates MEP and Michael Barratt Brown.
□ **ALLAN LARSSON MP** Can Europe Afford To Work? □ **KEN COATES MEP** The Dimensions of Recovery □ **MICHAEL BARRATT BROWN** Money, Debt & Slump □ **JACQUES DELORS** The Scope and Limits of Community Action □ **SIR DONALD MACDOUGALL** Economic and Monetary Union and the Community Budget □ **ANDREW MARVELL** Funding the Recovery Programme □ **STUART HOLLAND** Planning the Recovery Programme □ **PROF. WYNNE GODLEY** A Federal Government? □ **PROF. PETER TOWNSEND** What Hopes for European Social Policy? □ **FRANCIS CRIPPS & TERRY WARD** Employment Creation □ **MICHAEL BARRATT BROWN** Regional Recovery □ **REGAN SCOTT** Reforming Working Lifetimes □ **JOHN HUGHES** Linking Working Time with Recovery □ **KEN COATES MEP** Afterword: An Assize on Unemployment and Poverty? □

"It is vital that the debate about these and other ideas in the battle for jobs is taken out now to the people and our regional and local communities".

Ken Coates